WBI Development Studies

Granting and Renegotiating Infrastructure Concessions

Doing it Right

J. Luis Guasch

The World Bank
Washington, D.C.

The World Bank Institute was established by the World Bank in 1955 to train officials concerned with development planning, policymaking, investment analysis, and project implementation in member developing countries. At present the substance of WBI's work emphasizes macroeconomic and sectoral policy analysis. Through a variety of courses, seminars, workshops, and other learning activities, most of which are given overseas in cooperation with local institutions, WBI seeks to sharpen analytical skills used in policy analysis and to broaden understanding of the experience of individual countries with economic and social development. Although WBI's publications are designed to support its training activities, many are of interest to a much broader audience.

J. Luis Guasch is regional advisor on regulation and competitiveness, World Bank, Latin American and the Caribbean Region, and professor of economics, University of California, San Diego.

ISBN 0-8213-5792-1
e-ISBN 0-8213-5793-X

Library of Congress Cataloging-in-Publication Data has been applied for.

Contents

Foreword   vii

Preface   ix

Acknowledgments   xiii

1. Overview   1
    Infrastructure's Importance for Economic Growth   2
    Private Sector Participation and New Regulations and Risks   6
    Drawing on Experience to Improve Performance   9
    Outcomes of the Renegotiation Process   17
    Renegotiating Only When Justified   19

2. Options for Private Participation in Infrastructure   23
    Concessions—A Cancelable Right to Cash Flow   26
    Transferring Infrastructure Services to the Private Sector   26
    How Do Concessions Work?   27
    How Do Concessions Differ from Privatizations?   30
    Benefits of Concessions   31
    Drawbacks of Concessions   31
    Concession and Regulatory Design   32

3. Concessions and the Problem of Renegotiation   33
    Renegotiation Incidence and Incidents   34
    The Principle of Financial Equilibrium in Regulated Markets:
        More Regulation, More Renegotiation   35
    Bidding, Renegotiation, and Government Responses:
    Sanctity of the Bid   37
    The Case of Directly Adjudicated Concessions   39
    Other Drivers of Renegotiation   40

4. Anecdotal Evidence of the Drivers of Renegotiation   43
   Political and Institutional Issues   44
   Aggressive Bidding   44
   Faulty Contract Designs   48
   Government Failure to Honor Contract Clauses   60
   Defective Regulation and Its Effects   64
   Profile of a Typical Municipal Concession:
       Common Problems of Process and Design   65
   Macroeconomic Shocks   65

5. Renegotiation in Theory and Practice   71
   Reasons for Incomplete Contracts   71
   Incomplete Contracts, Concession Successes and Failures,
       and the Theory of Renegotiation   72
   Renegotiation Issues in Latin America and the Caribbean   77

6. Confirming Anecdote and Theory: Empirical Analysis
   of the Determinants of Renegotiation   79
   Basic Findings   80
   Empirical Analysis of the Determinants of Renegotiation   87
   Significant Variables Influencing the Incidence of Renegotiation   88
   Marginal Effects on the Probability of Renegotiation   90
   Interpretation of Empirical Results   90

7. Policy Implications and Lessons: Guidelines for Optimal
   Concession Design   95
   Shortcomings in Concession Designs and
       Regulations That Lead to Renegotiation   95
   Guidelines for Optimal Concession Design   96
   The Process for Awarding Concessions and Award Criteria   97
   Implementation of an Optimal Concession Award Criteria   101
   Financial Equilibrium Clauses for the Operation
       of the Concession in the Concession Contract   105
   Renegotiation Clauses and Triggers for Renegotiation   107
   Sanctity of the Bid   107
   Concession Length and Financing   107
   Investment Commitments   108
   Determining Future Tariffs   109
   Regulatory Structure: Rate of Return Versus Price Caps   111
   Cost of Capital and How It Should Be Determined   115
   Tariff and Revenue Implications of Increased Cost of Capital   120

Concession Risks and Their Allocation 121
Valuation of Concession Assets 121
Informational Requirements Set in the Concession Contract 127
Regulatory Accounting Norms 129
Addressing Termination of the Concession
      and Dispute Resolution 134
Arbitration Rules Stated in Concession Contract 135
Institutional Structure of Regulatory Agencies 135

8. Conclusion 141

Appendix 1. Data Description 149

Appendix 2. Choice and Definition of Independent Variables 157
Definition of Terms 157
Detailed Description of the Variables 161

Appendix 3. Econometric Analysis: Results of the Probit
   Estimations 167
      Summary Results 167
      Complete Estimates 171

References 183

Index 191

Foreword

This title is the fifth in an occasional series by the World Bank Institute intended to help meet the knowledge and information needs of infrastructure reformers and regulators. The book breaks new ground in relation to the design and implementation of concession contracts by culling the lessons of experience from some 1,000 examples and assessing what these lessons mean for future practice. The examples are taken from Latin America where, during the 1990s, governments throughout the region awarded contracts to the private sector to operate a range of public utilities, including electricity; water supply and sanitation; and airport, railway, and port services. The study shows the extent to which the concession award process, the contract design, the regulatory framework, and the overall governance structure tend to drive the success of any reform effort and the likelihood of contract renegotiation.

In assessing the concession process this book begins with the premise that the existing model and conceptual framework are appropriate, but that problems have arisen because of faulty designs and implementation. The book's main objectives are to aid in the design of future concessions and regulations and to contain the incidence of inappropriate renegotiation by means of thorough analysis and detailed policy lessons. The key issue is how to design better concession contracts and how to induce both parties to comply with the agreed upon terms of the concession to ensure long-term sector efficiency and vigorous network expansion.

The analysis has important policy implications. Indeed, the systematic analysis of this large dataset of concession contracts has highlighted specific reasons for the high rate of renegotiation of concessions, especially in transport and in water and sanitation. It shows how and why the best of intentions at the design stage can be counterproductive if the strategic behaviors of the key actors are not taken into account. The book provides guidelines for practitioners worldwide in crafting new concessions, renegotiating concessions, and identifying and avoiding problems.

This book is an essential tool for infrastructure reformers, regulators, and contract renegotiation teams and will help ensure that public-private partnerships are used in the most effective way to meet the infrastructure needs of the world's poorest.

Frannie A. Léautier, Vice President
World Bank Institute

Preface

Infrastructure services—electricity, water and sanitation, telecommunications, roads, railroads, ports, and airports—are critical to the operation and efficiency of a modern economy. They begin as critical inputs in the provision of goods and services and significantly affect the productivity, cost, and competitiveness of the economy and the alleviation of poverty. Poor infrastructure services often limit competitiveness in other markets, and limited coverage and access foster poverty. Policy decisions regarding their provision and sector development have ramifications throughout the economy.

Traditionally government-owned enterprises have provided infrastructure services. On average, however, government ownership has proven disappointing: increases in coverage have been limited, the quality of service has been deficient, and the levels of operational efficiency have been low. Moreover, to improve performance and coverage most state-owned enterprises urgently needed significant investment. Given the scarcity of public funds for investment and the competing needs in the social sectors, most countries have opted to transfer the provision of infrastructure services to the private sector. That transfer has often been accompanied by sector restructuring before the privatization or concessioning and by the implementation of a regulatory framework. Regulations serve both to protect investors from arbitrary and politically motivated intervention from the government and to protect users from the abuse of the monopoly or dominant position of the new private operators.

The need for that protection arises because, quite often, investments in infrastructure are sunk costs, that is, costs that cannot easily be recouped or salvaged if the economic atmosphere deteriorates. These high sunk costs may tempt governments to behave opportunistically, taking regulatory actions that expropriate the available quasi-rents once costs are sunk. When potential investors realize that this temptation exists, they may be discouraged from investing in the first place, unless the issue is properly addressed or unless an additional premium is required. That possibility is the main source of regulatory risk, affecting levels of investment, costs of capital, and tariffs, because additional premiums are required to cover that risk. Credible and stable regulation and transparent rules reduce that risk.

The government, however, is not the only entity that may behave opportunistically. Once an enterprise has been granted a concession or franchise in an infrastructure sector, that enterprise may correspondingly be able to take actions that "hold up" the government, for example, by insisting on renegotiating the regulatory contract ex post, or by regulatory capture to extract supranormal rents from the users, to the detriment of efficiency. The extensive informational advantages that the enterprise possesses over the government regulator (as well as over other potential operators) is one reason for this opportunism. If those issues are not addressed properly, the result may be a regulatory arrangement that is less effective than envisioned in protecting customers from monopoly abuses. Compounding the problem are the additional objectives to secure increased coverage, particularly of the poor, or to implement universal service. These objectives often do not mesh well with the natural incentives of private operators or, when provided through cross-subsidies, these objectives make the liberalization of the sector, with open competition through free entry, difficult.

Safeguards to limit that opportunism and to protect investors and users are usually built into the concession contract and the regulatory framework. How effective they have been is indeed a question and in part the motivation for this book.

The process of reform—concessioning operations to the private sector and setting up regulatory regimes and agencies—started in the mid-1980s in the Latin American and Caribbean region. These countries now have a wealth of experience on the performance of infrastructure concessions. Some countries in the region have been pioneers in implementing concessions as part of the structural reforms of their infrastructure sectors. Most of those concessions have had positive outcomes, showing extensive improvements in operating efficiency, in quality of service, and in service provision.

Yet a number of recurrent problems in the sectors, such as limited sharing by users of the efficiency gains, pervasive conflicts and renegotiations in the sectors, and weak regulatory effectiveness (for example, failure to understand that effective regulation is needed to achieve fair outcomes that benefit the poor) have raised concerns about the concessions model and led to calls for its evaluation. This book takes up that call by assessing the concession process, the regulatory framework, and their outcomes to determine the continued usefulness of the process for countries, investors, and users and to suggest needed adjustments. Among the main issues addressed are the design of concessions, the regulatory framework, the high incidence of contract renegotiation, and the implications for infrastructure performance and overall welfare. The premise is that the model and conceptual framework are appropriate, yet the problems have been in faulty design and implementation, and those can and should be improved.

The research driving this book was motivated by the perceived high incidence and quick concession contract renegotiations, especially the significant number seemingly motivated by opportunism on both sides, the government and the private operator. Many concession contracts have been renegotiated, affecting sector performance and welfare and compromising the credibility both of the reform program and of the countries involved. The book uses data from more than 1,000 concessions in infrastructure in Latin America and the Caribbean granted during 1985–2000, analyzing the incidence and determinants of renegotiation as a proxy for performance.

The book's main objectives are to aid in the design of future concessions and regulations and to contain the incidence of inappropriate renegotiation, through both thorough analysis and detailed policy lessons. Not all renegotiation is undesirable. In fact, some should be expected, and such efforts can improve welfare. Opportunistic renegotiation, however, should be discouraged in both existing and future concessions. The key issue is how to design better concession contracts and how to induce both parties to comply with the agreed-upon terms of the concession to secure long-term sector efficiency and vigorous network expansion.

To complement the findings here, a second phase of analysis is under way to compile performance indicators for the analyzed concessions. That effort will make evaluation of the impacts of renegotiated concessions possible and, more broadly, will allow imputation of the determinants of performance—not just renegotiation—such as efficiency, coverage, quality of service, and so on, in relation to many of the variables described here, including concession design, regulatory framework, country conditions, and the external environment.

Acknowledgments

The author is indebted to Soumya Chattopadhyay for invaluable assistance in compiling the dataset and developing the empirical analysis used in this book. He is also grateful to Antonio Estache for encouragement through the writing of this book and for comments and suggestions. In addition, the author would like to thank Roberto Chama, Paulo Correa, Eduardo Engel, Vivien Foster, Sue Goldmark, Tony Gomez-Ibañez, Gordon Hughes, Jose Luis Irigoyen, Michael Klein, Jean-Jacques Laffont, Danny Leipziger, S. C. Littlechild, Abel Mejia, Moises Naim, Martin Rodriguez-Pardina, Pablo Spiller, Jon Stern, Nick Stern, Joe Stiglitz, Stephane Straub, John Strong, and Carlos Velez for helpful comments. Partial financing from the Public–Private Infrastructure Advisory Facility is gratefully acknowledged. The excellent editorial assistance from Bruce Ross-Larsen is also acknowledged, as well as additional editing by The Word Doctor.

1

Overview

In most developing and industrial countries, infrastructure services have traditionally been provided by government enterprises, but in developing countries at least, these enterprises have often proven to be inefficient, unable to provide much-needed investments, and manipulated to achieve political objectives. By contrast, many studies have shown that over the past 30 years, private (or privatized) enterprises in developing countries have, on average, delivered superior performance and needed investments (Birdsall and Nellis 2002; Guasch, Andres, and Foster forthcoming; Kikeri and Nellis 2002; La Porta and Lopez-de-Silanes 1999; McKenzie and Mookherjee 2003; Megginson and Netter 2001; Nellis 2003; Torero and Pasco-Font 2001).

Explanations differ on why this discrepancy exists. Private enterprises are driven by a desire for profits and may have more professional know-how in management, operating procedures, and use of appropriate technology. But perhaps the most important reason for their stronger performance is that privatization makes intervening in enterprise operations difficult for governments and politicians, so government manipulation is less likely. However, the issue, in general, has been how to ensure that the improved performance and efficiency gains are passed through to the users through lower tariffs and increased coverage, while allowing firms to earn a fair rate of return on their investments. The failure of users to benefit from a significant share of those efficiency gains has been, to a large extent, the source of their discontent with the infrastructure reform programs in developing countries (Barja, McKenzie, and Urquiola 2002; Bitran and others 1999; Ennis and Pinto 2002; Estache 2003a,b; Estache, Gomez-Lobo, and Leipziger 2001; Freije and Rivas 2003; Lopez-Calva and Rosellon 2002; Macedo 2000; Navajas 2000; Ugaz and Waddams-Price 2003).

Private participation in infrastructure has also been driven by an urgent need for enormous investment. To improve infrastructure performance and coverage, most government enterprises would require significant new financing. Given scarce public funds and competing needs in the social sectors, most countries have instead opted to transfer the provision of infrastructure services to the private sector. Private participation can take a variety of forms, from management contracts to concessions (also in a variety of forms) to full privatization. When properly designed and implemented, all these forms have had significant success. At least in Latin America and the Caribbean, calls to the private sector to take over infrastructure services have attracted many bidders, but to secure concomitant improved sector performance, proper design of concession contracts and regulatory frameworks is essential.

Infrastructure's Importance for Economic Growth

Reforms to improve and extend infrastructure services have also been fueled by the realization in developing countries that infrastructure levels and quality have a huge effect on economic growth and poverty alleviation and that current levels and quality are inadequate. Infrastructure services are critical to the production and provision of goods and services and significantly affect an economy's productivity, costs, and competitiveness. Policies on the provision of infrastructure services reverberate throughout an economy—and poor services often limit competitiveness in other markets.

Numerous studies—including Calderon, Easterly, and Serven (2003a,b); Calderon and Serven (2003); Canning (1998); Reinikka and Svensson (1999); and World Bank (1994)—illustrate the impact of infrastructure on economic growth. A 1 percent increase in a country's level of just one type of infrastructure—such as telephone lines per worker—can increase gross domestic product (GDP) growth by 0.20 percentage points (table 1.1).

The level and quality of infrastructure in Latin America and the Caribbean improved between 1980 and 2000, but they remain deficient. Moreover, the region lost significant ground to East Asian and Organization for Economic Cooperation and Development countries (Calderon and Serven 2003). During 1980–97, the infrastructure gap between Latin America and East Asia grew by 40 percent for roads, 70 percent for telecommunications, and nearly 90 percent for power generation. Such gaps have enormous consequences. During 1980–2000, East Asia's GDP growth was almost twice Latin America's, and the widening infrastructure gap accounted for nearly

Table 1.1 *Effect on GDP Growth of a 1 Percent Increase in Infrastructure Assets*
(percent)

Type of asset	Direct effect	Indirect effect (via K)	Total effect
Power generation capacity per worker	0.07	0.02	0.09
Paved roads per worker	0.05	0.02	0.07
Telephone lines per worker	0.14	0.05	0.19

Note: The K effect refers to the impact via capital accumulation.
Source: Calderon and Serven (2003).

a quarter of GDP gap (table 1.2, figure 1.1). As figure 1.1 shows, the contribution of the infrastructure gap toward the output gap is considerable for
almost all countries in Latin America and the Caribbean.

Many studies at the microlevel have illustrated the effect of infrastructure on unit costs. For example, infrastructure levels and quality are strong
determinants of inventory levels. U.S. businesses typically hold inventories equal to about 15 percent of GDP, but inventories in many developing
countries, as I document here, are often twice as large, and raw materials
are often more than three times as large, as shown in table 1.3 (Guasch and
Kogan 2001, 2003). The impact of those inventory levels on firm unit costs
and on country competitiveness and productivity is extraordinarily significant. First are the financial costs associated with inventories, and those

Table 1.2 *The Impact on Growth of Latin America and the Caribbean's
Infrastructure Gap and Its Role in the Widening Output Gap with East Asia
and the Pacific, 1980–97*

Indicator	Amount
Change in the output gap between Latin America and East Asia (percentage change in log of relative GDP per worker)	91.9
Change in the output gap attributable to the growing infrastructure gap (percentage points, median of country data)	20.2
Share of the infrastructure gap in the output gap (percent)	22.0

Source: Calderon and Serven (2003).

Figure 1.1 *Contribution of the Infrastructure Gap to the Output Gap Relative to East Asia, 1980–97*
(percentage)

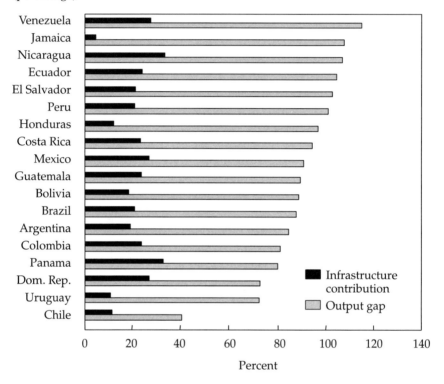

Source: Calderon and Serven (2003).

can be quite high, because the cost of capital in developing countries is usually well above 15 percent. Second are the other associated costs of inventories, such as taxes, insurance, obsolescence, and storage, that can add another 5 percentage points. Table 1.4, which illustrates the magnitude of those costs by value of inventory indicating an average cost of 19.25 percent and standard range for those costs between 9 and 50 percent, points out the urgency of lowering inventory levels. Putting things into perspective, if the interest rate for financing inventory holdings is 15–20 percent, a conservative estimate in most developing countries, then the cost to the economy of the additional inventory holdings is greater than 2 percent of GDP. Given the high cost of capital in most Latin American countries, the impact of that quasi-dead capital—the value of those inventories on unit

Table 1.3 *Latin America Inventories to U.S. Inventories Ratios, All Industries, 1990s*
(average of all available data)

Inventory ratio	Argentina	Bolivia	Brazil	Chile	Colombia	Ecuador	Mexico	Peru	Republica Bolivariana de Venezuela
Raw materials inventory									
Mean	3.10	4.20	2.98	2.17	2.22	5.06	1.58	4.19	2.82
Minimum	0.90	0.11	0.80	0.00	0.52	0.86	0.42	0.10	0.30
1st quartile	1.80	1.39	1.60	0.36	1.45	2.55	1.06	1.25	1.87
Median	2.20	2.90	2.00	1.28	1.80	3.80	1.36	2.30	2.61
3rd quartile	3.00	4.49	3.10	2.66	2.52	5.64	2.06	3.90	3.12
Maximum	9.30	34.97	7.10	68.92	13.59	20.61	3.26	31.10	7.21
Final goods inventory									
Mean	1.86	2.74	1.98	1.76	1.38	2.57	1.46	1.65	1.63
Minimum	0.74	0.11	0.75	0.01	0.19	0.67	0.35	0.39	0.10
1st quartile	1.20	1.13	1.10	0.17	1.05	1.67	0.82	1.17	0.87
Median	1.65	2.02	1.60	0.72	1.28	1.98	1.36	1.54	1.60
3rd quartile	2.10	3.18	2.00	1.38	1.63	2.86	2.14	2.11	2.14
Maximum	6.50	21.31	5.20	31.61	5.31	7.94	4.91	3.87	5.29

Source: Guasch and Kogan (2001).

Table 1.4 Inventory Carrying Cost Components

Component	Average (percent)	Range (percent)
Capital cost	15.00	8.0–40
Taxes	1.00	0.5–2
Insurance	0.05	0–1
Obsolescence	1.20	0.5–3
Storage	2.00	0–4
Total	19.25	9.0–50

Source: Bowersox and Closs (1996).

costs and productivity or competitiveness—is enormous. And a key determinant is not interest rates, as classical models predict, but poor infrastructure (roads and ports). A one-standard-deviation improvement of infrastructure decreases raw material inventories by 20–40 percent (Guasch and Kogan 2003).

Likewise logistic costs, as reported in Guasch (2002), are significantly high in Latin American and Caribbean countries, ranging as shown in figure 1.2, from a low for Chile of 15 percent of value product to a high in Peru of 34 percent. The Organization for Economic Cooperation and Development countries average hovers around 10 percent. Again a key determinant of those high logistic costs is poor infrastructure, especially roads, ports, and telecommunications (Guasch and Hahn 1999). Thus infrastructure matters significantly for productivity or competitiveness and growth. Finally the large impact of infrastructure on poverty has also been widely documented (see Brook and Irwin 2003; Chisari, Estache, and Romero 1999; Estache, Foster, and Woodon 2002).

Private Sector Participation and New Regulations and Risks

Recognizing infrastructure's importance and, as noted, lacking sufficient funds, most developing countries have turned to the private sector to finance and operate infrastructure services, seeking investment and know-how to accelerate improvements in service levels and quality. Private participation is often preceded by sector restructuring and by new laws and regulations. Such efforts are intended to protect investors from politically motivated government intervention, to protect users from the abuse of

Figure 1.2 *Logistics Costs as a Percentage of Product Value, 2000*

Percent

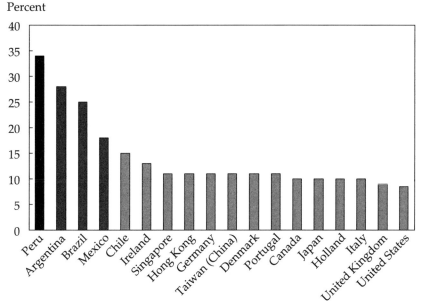

Source: Guasch (2002).

monopoly or dominant positions by new private operators (because many infrastructure services have components of natural monopolies), and to ensure competition between new entrants and dominant incumbent operators when feasible. Required investments are often highly specific sunk costs—that is, costs that cannot easily be recouped if the economic atmosphere deteriorates or if the operator discontinues operations and that cannot be used for other activities.

These high sunk costs may tempt governments to behave opportunistically, taking regulatory actions that expropriate rents once costs are sunk, such as compulsory or unilateral renegotiations of agreed-upon contract terms. A typical scenario is a government (or mayors in the case of water concessions, because they usually have exclusive jurisdiction) seeking to secure popular support during a reelection campaign and deciding to cut tariffs or not honor agreed-upon tariff increases. Another common scenario is a new administration (or mayor) deciding not to honor tariff increases agreed to in a concession contract granted by a previous administration or pursuing different priorities than the previous administration and so requesting a different action plan. Investors, aware of such pitfalls, might avoid investing in the first place unless such issues are properly addressed, or they may require an additional premium (higher tariffs, smaller transfer fees) to account for the risk.

Depending on the country and sector, such regulatory risks can add 2–6 percentage points to the cost of capital (Guasch and Spiller 2001). Higher tariffs or lower transfer fees or sale prices are then needed to cover these higher costs. For example, a 5 percentage point increase in the cost of capital to account for regulatory risks will reduce an offered transfer fee or sale price by 35 percent or require a 20 percent increase in tariffs. For a specific case, in the water concession in Buenos Aires, Argentina, the regulator grants a 3.5 percent increase in tariffs for each 1 percentage point increase in the cost of capital.

Governments are not the only parties who may behave opportunistically. Once a private enterprise has been granted a concession in an infrastructure sector, it may be able to "hold up" the government—for example, by insisting on renegotiating the contract, seeking more favorable terms, or using regulatory capture.[1] An enterprise's extensive information advantages over government (and, in most cases, over other potential operators) and perceived leverage in negotiations can give it strong incentives to renegotiate a contract and secure a better deal than the original bid. The resulting regulatory arrangements may be less effective in protecting customers from monopoly abuses. Thus the design of regulations, concession and privatization contracts, and implementation agreements can significantly affect sector performance and the incidence of renegotiation (Fundación de Investigaciones Económicas Latinoamericanas 1999; Gomez-Ibanez 2003; Guasch and Spiller 2001; Manzetti 2000).

Moreover, neutral events not induced by governments or service providers—for example, internal or external macroeconomic shocks such as the sharp devaluations in Mexico in 1994, Brazil in 1999, and Argentina in 2001—can significantly undermine the financial equilibrium of firms, because for infrastructure services, revenues are collected in local currency but investments, equity, and debt are usually in foreign currency such as U.S. dollars (for an illustration see Benitez, Chisari, and Estache 2003). The impact of such events should be addressed, as much as possible, in spelled-out contingencies in the contract and also by guidelines for the

---

1. Regulatory capture means the operator or concessionaire unduly secures influence—overt or covert—over the regulatory process to bias the regulator's decisions in favor of the interests of the operator or concessionaire.

process and substance of the adjustment in the concession contracts. In the renegotiation induced by such events, however, negotiators should be careful to avoid improperly reallocating rents to either party. The possibility of such neutral events—and the fact that concession contracts often do not provide clear guidelines on how to respond to them—also increase regulatory risks. Thus, as much as possible, contracts should provide clear guidelines for adjustments in such conditions.

Barring major unforeseen events, and others that can be spelled in the contract as contingencies, the key issues are, first, the design of a proper concession, regulatory framework, and contractual arrangements and, second, how to increase the likelihood that both signatory parties to a concession contract comply with terms of the contract and avoid opportunistic renegotiation. A key start is the design of better contracts that do not facilitate renegotiation and that penalize noncompliance.

Drawing on Experience to Improve Performance

After nearly 20 years of experience, countries have no excuse for most errors in the design and implementation of concessions and related regulations. Faulty design and implementation have significant implications for both efficiency and equity, affecting general perceptions of the validity of concessions. Moreover, many such problems can be corrected relatively easily.

In many Latin American and Caribbean countries, perceptions are widespread that privatization and concession programs have been unfair and have benefited the wealthy and hurt the poor through job losses and higher tariffs and that processes have lacked transparency, proceeds have been misused, efficiency gains secured by operators have not been shared by the users, and corruption has run rampant.

Many studies have evaluated the performance of those infrastructure reform programs and showed significant improvements, but they also point out problems and perhaps fuel perceptions (for a review of the theory see Coelli and others 2003, and for illustrations see Estache, Gonzalez, and Trujillo 2002a, b). In particular, a number of studies evaluate efficiency gains of concessioned firms, showing significant annual gains, ranging from 1–9 percent (see Estache, Guasch, and Trujillo 2003 for a summary), but they also report at best a weak correlation with tariff changes. The intended objectives and expectations of the concession and regulatory framework were to provide incentives for firms to secure efficiency gains particularly through price-cap regulatory regimes. Through proper regulation, according to the design objective, those efficiency gains would be passed to the users via lower tariffs. Table 1.5 illustrates a case of the lack of sharing of

Table 1.5 *Comparing Annual Real Tariff Changes since Privatization and Concession with Efficiency Gains in Argentina*
(percent)

Indicator	Electricity distribution	Gas distribution	Water distribution	Telecommunications service
Evidence of the poor correlation between average tariffs and efficiency changes				
Annual average tariff change	–0.75	–0.8	+1.75 (for Aguas Argentinas)	–0.6
Approximation of annual efficiency gains used in tariff revision	1 (shift)	2.9 (shift + average catching up)	6.1 (shift + average catching up for four water companies)	3.9 (shift + catching up)
Evidence of the increased share of rent allocated to the government rather than to the users				
Indirect tax	20–57	20–30	20–30	40–50

Source: Estache, Guasch, and Trujillo (2003).

efficiency gains by users in Argentina. Although efficiency gains were large, ranging from 1 to 6 percent, tariff decreases were quite low, less than 1 percent. In some cases, such as in the water sector, tariffs increased, but the government did keep a share of those efficiency gains, directly benefiting, through increased tax revenues.

Reinforcing the argument that efficiency gains were seldom passed through the users are the claims that many new private operators have fared quite well on their investments and that government tax revenues from operators have been significant. Preliminary evidence from Foster and others (2003) in an ongoing study of the profitability of private participation in infrastructure in Latin America shows that, on average, during the 1990s, the internal rate of return (IRR) was significantly above the cost of equity for telecommunications operations, about the same for energy operations, and below the cost of equity for water and sanitation operations, although the variance is large and a number of firms have not fared well (table 1.6).[2] That weak or absent correlation between efficiency gains and

Table 1.6 *Average Profitability by Sector of Privatized and Concessioned Firms and the Cost of Equity in Latin American and Caribbean Countries, 1990–2000* (percent)

Sector	IRR (adjusted)[a]	Initial cost of equity[b]
Telecommunications	26.8	14.0
Water and sanitation	13.0	15.5
Energy	14.0	14.0

a. The IRR has been adjusted to incorporate management fees.
b. Cost of equity is evaluated at the time of the transaction.
Source: Foster and others (2003).

2. To measure the overall return that shareholders in a specific project earned on the capital they invested in that project and then determine if that return is appropriate given the risk they took, one computes the IRR they made on their investment and compares it with the cost of equity (C_E) in the country and sector of investment. The project IRR is the return earned by investors in the project from flows of dividends minus flows of capital injections into the project over the life of the project. Mathematically it is the return that brings to zero the net present value of the net flows earned by the project shareholders on their investment, that is, dividends minus capital injections. The cost of equity is a measure of the appropriate return that investors should expect on equity investments in a specific country and sector, given the level of risk of such investments.

lower tariffs and the perceived profitability of the private operators, often secured through additional benefits captured through renegotiation, have been at the core of the increasing dissatisfaction among users.

According to a late 2001 survey by Latinobarometro, 63 percent of people in 17 countries in Latin America and the Caribbean believed that privatizations of state companies had not been beneficial, up from 57 percent in 2000 and 43 percent in 1998 (McKenzie and Mookherjee 2003). Such negative perceptions have achieved enough momentum to delay private participation in infrastructure in Peru, to abort its start in Ecuador, and to threaten to backtrack the process in Bolivia and elsewhere.[3] These concerns must be addressed and resolved through a systematic evaluation of the concessions process to draw lessons for improvement—the motivation for this book.

To a large extent these negative sentiments are driven by the high incidence of renegotiation and the responses to it. Renegotiation implies a lack of compliance with agreed-upon terms and departures from expected promises of sector improvements. On average, the outcome of renegotiations adversely affected the users.

Renegotiation has occurred if a concession contract underwent a significant change or amendment not envisioned or driven by stated contingencies in any of the following areas: tariffs, investment plans and levels, exclusivity rights, guarantees, lump-sum payments or annual fees, coverage targets, service standards, and concession periods. Standard scheduled tariff adjustments and periodic tariff reviews are not considered renegotiations.

To illustrate the problematic of renegotiation of concessions, this overview presents a number of key summary statistics from the compiled dataset of more than 1,000 concessions granted in the Latin American and Caribbean region during 1985–2000.

Renegotiation was extremely common among the concessions in the sample, occurring in 30 percent of them (table 1.7). Not including the concessions in the telecommunications sector, because practically all telecommunications projects were privatized rather than concessioned, raises the incidence of renegotiation to 41.5 percent. Renegotiation was especially

---

3. Examples of ineffective concessions include highway concessions in Mexico; water concessions in Tucuman and Buenos Aires, Argentina, and Cochabamba, Bolivia; build-operate-transfer water concessions in Mexico; electricity distribution concessions in Arequipa, Peru; and railroad concessions in Colombia.

Table 1.7 *Incidence of Renegotiation, Total and by Sector*

Incidence of renegotiation	Total	Total (excluding telecom- munications)	Electricity	Transpor- tation	Water and sanitation
Percentage of renegotiated contracts	30	41.5	9.7	54.7	74.4

Source: Author's calculations.

common in transportation concessions, occurring in 55 percent of concessions, and even more so in water and sanitation concessions, occurring in 74 percent of concessions.

Renegotiation was far less common in telecommunications and energy, to some extent as a result of the more competitive nature of these sectors. That competitive nature significantly reduces the leverage of concessionaires and bargaining power for renegotiations. In most cases, telecommunications and energy concessionaires are not the only service providers, so governments have more options for securing these services from other operators in the event of a threat by operators to abandon the concessions if renegotiation demands were not met.

Most renegotiated concessions underwent renegotiation very soon after their award, with an average of just 2.2 years between concession awards and renegotiations (table 1.8). Renegotiations came most quickly in water and sanitation concessions, occurring an average of 1.6 years after concession awards. Renegotiations of transportation concessions occurred after an average of 3.1 years, perhaps reflecting the sector's longer construction times. Moreover, the variance in the distribution of renegotiation periods was small, with 85 percent of renegotiations occurring within 4 years of concession awards and 60 percent occurring within 3 years—for concessions that were supposed to run for 15–30 years (table 1.9).

Contract Award

Most of the concessions in the sample were awarded through competitive bidding rather than through direct adjudication and bilateral negotiation (table 1.10). But renegotiation was far less likely in concessions awarded noncompetitively, occurring in just 8 percent of such contracts—compared

Table 1.8 *Average Time to Renegotiate since Award, Mid-1980s to 2000* (years)

All renegotiated concessions	Transportation sector only	Water and sanitation sector only
2.2	3.1	1.6

Source: Author's calculations.

Table 1.9 *Small Variance of Time Distribution to Renegotiate, Mid-1980s to 2000*

Time distribution to renegotiation	Percentage of renegotiated contracts
Within first 4 years after concession award	85
Within first 3 years after concession award	60

Source: Author's calculations.

Table 1.10 *Contract Award Processes for Concessions in Latin America and the Caribbean by Sector, Mid-1980s to 2000*

Award process	Tele-communications	Energy	Trans-porta-tion	Water and sanitation	Total	Share of total (percent)
Competitive bidding	245	95	231	125	696	78
Direct adjudication (bilateral negotiation)	15	143	37	4	199	22
Total	260	238	268	129	895	100

Source: Author's calculations.

with 46 percent for contracts awarded through competitive bidding (excluding telecommunications concessions, table 1.11). The explanation is that for a number of reasons bilateral negotiation allows the operator to extract much more favorable concession terms, and that flexibility lessens the incentives for renegotiation.

Table 1.11 *Percentage of Concessions Renegotiated According to Competitive or Noncompetitive Process Excluding the Telecommunications Sector*

Incidence of renegotiation by type of process	Frequency
Renegotiation when awarded via competitive bidding	46
Renegotiation when awarded via bilateral negotiations	8

Source: Author's calculations.

Type of Regulation

Most concessions, 56 percent, were regulated through a price-cap regime. About 20 percent of the concessions were regulated through a rate-of-return regime, and about 24 percent had a hybrid regime (table 1.12).

Initiator of Renegotiation

In 61 percent of cases, concessionaries requested renegotiation, and in 26 percent of the cases, the government initiated renegotiation (table 1.13). In the remaining cases both the concessionaire and the government jointly sought renegotiation. When conditioned by the type of regulatory regime in place (table 1.14), one can see that operators were predominantly and almost exclusively the initiators of renegotiation (83 percent), but under a rate-of-return regime, the government led the request for renegotiation, although with a much lower incidence (34 percent). That figure is partially explained by the increased risk to the operator of a price-cap regulatory regime.

Table 1.12 *Distribution of Concessions by Type of Regulation*
(percent)

Type of regulation	Frequency
Price cap	56
Rate of return	20
Hybrid[a]	24

a. Hybrid regimes are defined when, under a price-cap regulatory regime, a large number of cost components are allowed an automatic pass-through into tariff adjustments.
Source: Author's calculations.

Table 1.13 *Who Initiated the Renegotiation?*
(percentage of total requests)

Sector	Both government and operator	Government	Operator
All sectors	13	26	61
Water and sanitation	10	24	66
Transportation	16	27	57

Source: Author's calculations.

Investment Obligations

Most concessions, 73 percent, had investment obligations that had to be met by the operator, and only about 21 percent were required to comply with performance or output indicators only. About 6 percent had both investment obligations and output indicators (table 1.15).

Contract Features and the Incidence of Renegotiation

Renegotiation was far more likely (renegotiation occurred in 60 in percent of cases) when concession contract awards were based on the lowest proposed tariff rather than on the highest transfer fee (11 percent); see table 1.16. Renegotiation was also much more likely when concession contracts contained investment requirements (70 percent) than when they included performance indicators (18 percent). Moreover, the incidence of renegotiation was much higher under price-cap regulation (42 percent) than rate-of-return regulation (13 percent), and when a regulatory agency was not in place (61 percent) than when one was in place (17 percent). Finally, renegotiation was more likely when the regulatory framework was embedded in the contract (40 percent) than when embedded in a decree (28 percent) or a law (17 percent).

Table 1.14 *Who Initiated the Renegotiation Conditioned on Regulatory Regime?*
(percentage of total requests)

Regulatory regime	Both government and operator	Government	Operator
Price cap	11	6	83
Rate of return	39	34	26
Hybrid regime	30	26	44

Source: Author's calculations.

Table 1.15 *Distribution of Concessions by Existence of Investment Obligations in Contract*
(percent)

Investment obligations versus performance indicators in concession contracts	Percentage of contracts
Investment obligations in contract	73
No investment obligations in contract but performance indicators	21
Hybrid	6

Source: Author's calculations.

Table 1.16 *Contract Features and the Incidence of Renegotiated Concessions in Latin America and the Caribbean, Mid-1980s to 2000*

Feature	Incidence of renegotiation (percent)
Award criteria	
Lowest tariff	60
Highest transfer fee	11
Regulation criteria	
Investment requirements (regulation by means)	70
Performance indicators (regulation by objectives)	18
Regulatory framework	
Price cap	42
Rate of return	13
Existence of regulatory body	
Regulatory body in existence	17
Regulatory body not in existence	61
Impact of legal framework	
Regulatory framework embedded in law	17
Regulatory framework embedded in decree	28
Regulatory framework embedded in contract	40

Source: Author's calculations.

Outcomes of the Renegotiation Process

The main issues in the renegotiation process were not surprising: tariff adjustments, investment obligations and their schedule, cost components that were to be automatically passed through to tariffs, adjustments on the annual fee—usually based on revenues—paid by the operator to the government, changes in the asset base to impute rate of return and extension of concession contracts. The common argument used by operators for soliciting the renegotiation of the concession contract was an imbalance in the financial equilibrium of the concession contract because of a number of factors. By contrast, the main arguments used by governments when requesting an renegotiation of the contract have been changes in government priorities in the sector, political concerns (often linked to the electoral cycle), dissatisfaction with the level and speed of sector development, and noncompliance by operator with agreed-upon terms. Table 1.17 shows the incidence and direction of adjustments of those components in the outcome of renegotiation. Note that on average, renegotiation tended to favor the operator, securing increases in tariffs (62 percent), delays and decreases in investment obligations (69 percent), increases in the number of cost components with an automatic pass-through to tariffs (59 percent), and decreases in the annual fee paid by the operator to the government (31 percent). A small number of renegotiations, however, led to tariff decreases (19 percent), increases in the annual fee paid by the operator to the government (17 percent), and unfavorable changes for the operator of the asset base (22 percent).

Table 1.17 *Common Outcomes of the Renegotiation Process*

Renegotiation outcome	*Percentage of renegotiated concession contracts with that outcome*
Delays on investment obligations targets	69
Acceleration of investment obligations	18
Tariff increases	62
Tariff decreases	19
Increase in the number of cost components with an automatic pass-through to tariff increases	59
Extension of concession period	38
Reduction of investment obligations	62
Adjustment of canon—annual fee paid by operator to government	
Favorable to operator	31
Unfavorable to operator	17
Changes in the asset-capital base	
Favorable to operator	46
Unfavorable to operator	22

Source: Author's calculations.

Renegotiating Only When Justified

In principle, renegotiation can be a positive instrument when it addresses the inherently incomplete nature of concession contracts. Properly used, renegotiation can enhance welfare. Although some renegotiation is desirable, appropriate, and to be expected, this high incidence exceeds expected and reasonable levels and raises concerns about the validity of the concession model. It might even indicate excessively opportunistic behavior by new operators or by governments. Such behavior undermines the efficiency of the process and the overall welfare, because renegotiation takes place between the government and the operator only, so it is not subject to competitive pressures and their associated discipline. When used opportunistically or strategically by an operator or government, to secure additional benefits, and not driven by the incompleteness of a contract, renegotiation can undermine the integrity of a concession, reduce welfare, and threaten the desired structural reform program in infrastructure. The high incidence of renegotiation reported here should indeed be a cause of concern.

Renegotiation, particularly opportunistic renegotiation, can reduce or eliminate the expected benefits of competitive bidding. If the auction is designed well and provides adequate incentives, competitive bidding for the right to operate a concession for a given number of years should elicit the most efficient operator. If bidders believe that renegotiation is feasible and likely, however, their incentives and bidding will be effected, and the auction will likely select, not the most efficient provider, but the one most skilled at renegotiations. Renegotiation should occur only when justified by the initial contract's built-in contingencies or by major unexpected events. The objective is to improve the design of concessions to secure long-term sector efficiency, fostering compliance with the terms agreed to by both the government and the operator. To establish such an environment, concession laws and contracts should include the elements listed below. Concession contract elements can be grouped into two categories: (a) those required to design contracts that focus on securing long-term sector efficiency and discourage opportunistic bidding and renegotiation, and (b) those required to implement regulations that impede opportunistic renegotiation and force contract compliance.

Good design includes the following concession contract elements:

- Concession contracts should be awarded competitively and designed to avoid ambiguities as much as possible. Contracts should clearly define the treatment of assets, evaluation of investments, outcome indicators, procedures and guidelines to adjust and review tariffs, and criteria and penalties for early termination of concession and procedures for resolution of conflicts.

- Concession contracts should contain clauses committing governments to a policy of no renegotiation except in the case of well-defined triggers. They should stipulate the process for and level of adjustments. The contract should specify that the operators will be held to their submitted bids. This approach forces operators to bear the costs of aggressive bids and of normal commercial risks—even if doing so results in the abandonment of concessions. In addition, the first tariff review should not be entertained for a significantly long period (at least five years) unless contract contingencies are triggered.
- Concession contracts should provide for significant compensation to operators in the event of unilateral changes to the contract by the government, including penalties.
- Consideration should be given to making operators pay a significant fee for any renegotiation request. If the renegotiation is decided in the operator's favor, the fee would be reimbursed.
- Detailed analysis of seemingly aggressive bids—or at least of the top two bids, particularly if they differ significantly—should be required before a concession is awarded. And if the financial viability of aggressive bids appears highly dubious, a mechanism should be in place to allow those bids to be disqualified or to increase the performance bond significantly in relation to the difference between the bids. In any case, operators should be required to post performance bonds of significant value.
- Claims for renegotiation should be reviewed as transparently as possible, possibly through external, professional panels to assist regulators and governments in their analysis and decisionmaking. Any adjustments granted should be explained to the public as quickly as possible.

Good implementation includes the following contract elements:

- Hurried, quickly organized concession programs should be avoided. Such an approach might secure more transactions, but it also leads to less satisfactory outcomes.
- Infrastructure concessions should be awarded through competitive bidding—rather than direct adjudication or bilateral negotiation—

and only after contracts have been carefully designed and reviewed and the qualifications of bidders have been screened.

- An appropriate regulatory framework and agency should be in place prior to the award of concessions, with sufficient autonomy and implementation capacity to ensure high-quality enforcement and to deter political opportunism. In addition, the tradeoffs between types of regulation—price cap and rate of return—should be well understood, including their different allocations of risk and implications for renegotiation. Technical regulation should fit information requirements and existing risks, and regulation should be by objectives and not by means. Thus performance objectives should be used instead of investment obligations.

- Proper regulatory accounting of all assets and liabilities should also be in place, to avoid any ambiguity about the regulatory treatment and allocation of cost, investments, asset base, revenues, transactions with related parties, management fees, and operational and financial variables. To ensure consistency, lock-in effects, and adequate tariffs, contracts should generally be awarded on the basis of the highest proposed transfer fee rather than the lowest proposed tariff.[4] Finally, outcome targets (regulation by objectives) should be the norm in contracts rather than investment obligations (regulation by means)

---

4. The least present value of revenues criteria developed by Engel, Fischer, and Galetovic (2001) should be strongly considered for road concessions, given its built-in incentives deterring renegotiation.

2

Options for Private Participation in Infrastructure

In the mid-1980s many developing countries, starting in Latin America and the Caribbean, initiated significant economic reforms. A large component of those reforms involved allowing private sector participation in the provision of infrastructure services, transferring from governments to private enterprises significant parts of the management and control of utility operations. These private enterprises were either existing individual corporate entities or consortiums of such entities (foreign and domestic) formed to provide these services. The drive to bring in private sector participation was motivated by the desire and need to improve sector performance and to secure much needed investments that the public sector was unable to provide because of the scarcity of public funds and competing investment needs in the social sectors.

Many types of private participation occur in the provision of infrastructure services (figure 2.1). Each type differs in terms of government participation levels, risk allocations, investment responsibilities, operational requirements, and incentives for operators (table 2.1). The most common types are privatizations and concessions and, to a much lesser extent, management contracts.

In sectors such as telecommunications, and to some extent electricity generation and natural gas (the usual pioneer sectors for private sector participation), private sector participation has generally been achieved through outright privatization—that is, divestiture accompanied by structural reforms of market structures and regulations. But in other sectors— ports, airports, roads, railroads, water and sanitation , and segments of the

Figure 2.1 *Types of Private Participation in Infrastructure*

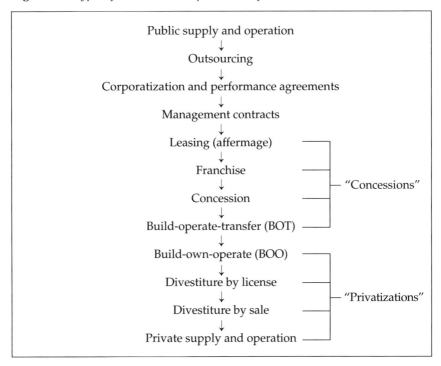

Source: Guasch (2002).

electricity sector—legal, political, and constitutional restraints have impeded the sale of public utilities to private parties (which are often foreign companies, making the issue even more complicated politically).

Moreover, in some countries that have no legal or constitutional impediments to full privatization of infrastructure services, concerns about performance have led governments to retain some control in various sectors. Thus in many countries where the state could not or did not want to transfer ownership of public assets to the private sector, innovative strategies have been used to introduce private participation in infrastructure. Among the alternatives to outright privatization, concessions for the right to operate a service for a defined period have emerged as the leading approach. In Latin America and the Caribbean, concessions have been especially common for water and sanitation and transportation services (table 2.2). As elsewhere, outright divestiture has been the preferred mode for telecommunications.

Table 2.1 *Jurisdictions and Responsibilities under Different Types of Private Participation*

Variable	Management contracts	Concessions	Privatizations
Ownership of physical and land assets	Government	Government	Private operator
Ownership of vehicles	Government	Government/ private operator	Private operator
Investment responsibilities	Government	Private operator	Private operator
Service control	Government	Government/ private operator	Government/ private operator
Tariff control	Government	Government/ private operator	Government/ private operator
Revenue risk	Government	Private operator	Private operator
Cost risk	Government	Private operator	Private operator
Labor risk	Government	Private operator	Private operator
Management cost risk	Private operator	Private operator	Private operator

Source: Author's compilation.

Table 2.2 *Incidence of Concessions in Infrastructure Projects Involving Private Participation in Latin America and the Caribbean, 1990–2000*

Sector	Number of projects	Number of concessions	Concessions as share of all projects (percentage)
Water and sanitation	91	81	89
Transportation	281	274	98
Energy	364	198	54
Telecommunications	113	3	3
Total	849	553	65

Source: World Bank, private participation in infrastructure database 2002.

Concessions—A Cancelable Right to Cash Flow

Concessions grant a private firm the right to operate a defined infrastructure service and to receive revenues deriving from it, usually based on a competitive bidding process. Concessions are typically granted for a specified period to the firm that offers to provide the service on the best terms while meeting certain criteria, generally involving quality and investment.

Concessions also include greenfield (brand new) projects such as build-operate-transfer (BOT) contracts, a standard feature of the energy sector that is becoming more common in other infrastructure sectors. A common approach is one in which concessionaires finance investments in exchange for long-term purchase (off-take) agreements for 80–90 percent of a facility's capacity. The development of power plants and gas transmission pipelines by independent operators (those not part of vertically integrated utilities) rely heavily on such arrangements. BOT contracts have also been used for large water supply systems (such as reservoirs), transmission pipelines, water treatment plants, and sewage treatment.

Transferring Infrastructure Services to the Private Sector

The transfer of public infrastructure services to the private sector—whether through a privatization or a concession—typically involves the following (see Newbery 2000 for a detailed and lucid exposition):

- *Sector restructuring and unbundling*, in which state companies are broken down (unbundled) to facilitate competition and reduce potential abuses of monopoly powers or dominant positions. Vertical and horizontal restrictions are often imposed, again to preempt abuses of dominant positions and promote strategic use of essential facilities.
- *Regulatory reform*, in which regulations are implemented and regulatory agencies are established to restrict natural monopoly advantages and to protect users from monopolistic behavior and investors from arbitrary government action.
- *Prequalification*, which sets basic technical or economic conditions (or both) that competing private operators must fulfill to be eligible for the bidding and selection processes.
- *Competitive bidding or an auction mechanism* to dissipate monopoly rents and select the most efficient operator among interested private operators.

- *Award of the concession contract* to one of the private operators based on selection criteria.
- *Concession contract components,* including stipulations for its duration, investment requirements, quality and service parameters, revenue sources, regulatory provisions, frequency of tariff adjustments and review processes, and transfer of assets on contract termination or conclusion.
- *Concession contract enforcement and regulatory oversight,* which are provided by the regulatory agency if it exists; if not, then by the sector ministry.

How Do Concessions Work?

Concession contracts are typically defined by four features as follows:

- The contract governs the relationship between the concession-granting authority and the private concessionaire.[1] The concession-granting authority is the government, an interministerial commission, or less common—and least appropriate—the regulatory agency.
- The concession is awarded for a limited but potentially renewable period. During this period the concessionaire enjoys the exclusive right to use the assets, exploit existing facilities, and develop new ones. The contract determines the conditions and prices at which the concessionaire provides the service and uses these facilities, which continue to be publicly owned.
- The concessionaire is responsible for all investments and for developing all new facilities—many of which are specified in the contract—under the supervision of the state or regulator. The concessionaire retains control and use rights over the new assets until they are handed over at the expiration of the contract. The contract might contain a clause specifying compensation for investments not fully amortized by the end of the concession period, and clauses specifying causes and remedies for early termination of contract and stating penalties and fines for noncompliance with agreed-upon terms.

---

1. The book uses the terms concessionaire and operator interchangeably, meaning the private party operating the concession.

- The concessionaire is remunerated based on contractually established tariffs (with appropriate guidelines for review and adjustment) collected directly from users. These prices are typically regulated through rate-of-return or price-cap mechanisms, usually driven by the principle of "efficient financial equilibrium"—allowing the firm to earn a fair rate of return on its investments. If revenues do not cover costs, compensation mechanisms are established (see Kerf and others 1998 for more details on concession features).

Given the wide range of settings in which they are used, however, concessions are often far more complicated than these basic features suggest. Concession contracts also usually contain other obligations and rights that require regular regulatory oversight in monitoring compliance, reconciling interpretations, adjusting tariffs, periodic (usually quinquennial) tariff reviews, and renegotiating triggers and terms (when appropriate and in light of experience). Government's role then involves setting rules for competition at the bidding stage and enforcing terms of agreements and compliance with regulations (box 2.1).

The duration of concession contracts tends to (and usually should) reflect the number of years that investors require to recoup their investments, although setting the time to secure full amortization might not be essential or possible. Infrastructure services require continuous investments that cannot be predicted decades in advance, and investments almost always must made toward the end of the contract and cannot be amortized before its expiration. Moreover, the true value of the business includes the incumbent's unamortized assets and such intangibles as know-how and reputation. Thus contracts should provide incentives to maintain all service-related facilities throughout the life of the concession.

For example, a government could pay a private operator based on an evaluation by an independent expert. Or a concession could be re-bid periodically, as Argentina has done in the power sector—where concessions are for 95 years but are re-bid after the first 15 years and then after every 10 years. If the incumbent outbids its opponents, it retains control. If not, it relinquishes control but is compensated for outstanding investments. In monopolistic sectors even BOO schemes need not imply permanence. Although the private company owns the assets indefinitely, to provide the service it often needs an operating license that the government can revoke at any time (subject to certain conditions and stipulated compensation).

Because all possible contingencies cannot be accounted for in regulations and concession contracts, concessions may provide regulators with

Box 2.1 *A Sample of Government Responsibilities for Concessions*

Framework
- Adopting legal provisions to enable the granting of concessions
- Establishing or identifying regulatory authorities
- Managing government support to infrastructure projects
- Managing public relations and information.

Project identification and analysis
- Identifying and prioritizing projects amenable to concessions
- Hiring advisers
- Performing a preliminary review of project costs and benefits (without duplicating the analysis to be performed by the private sector), especially in cases where the government will be assuming some of the market risk
- Reviewing legal and regulatory issues
- Determining preliminary selection criteria
- Granting permission for the project to go ahead (for example, for the opening of the bidding process)
- Setting a timetable for the project.

Enabling and supporting measures
- Granting permits and other necessary authorizations (such as rights of way and environmental permits)
- Determining the form of government support for the project.

Design of concession arrangements
- Choosing legal instruments
- Allocating responsibilities
- Choosing and designing pricing rules and performance targets
- Determining bonuses and penalties
- Determining duration and termination
- Designing adaptation mechanisms to new or unforeseen circumstances
- Choosing and designing dispute settlement mechanisms.

Concession award
- Choosing the award method
- Making decisions about prequalification and shortlisting
- Determining bid structure and evaluation method
- Determining bidding rules and procedures
- Proceeding with the bidding
- Negotiating.

Exercise of regulatory function through autonomous regulatory agency
- Implementing regulatory rules
- Supervising and monitoring
- Enforcing rules (for example, imposing penalties).

Source: Kerf and others (1998).

some discretion—while providing concessionaires with some recourse and appeal in the event of perceived inappropriate requirements. Whatever the approach, all concessions require oversight and some type of regulation.

How Do Concessions Differ from Privatizations?

Although concessions and privatizations tend to achieve the same objectives—securing private sector managerial and operational expertise and investments—they differ in three key respects. First, concessions do not involve the sale or transfer of ownership of physical assets, only of the right to use the assets and to operate the enterprise. Second, concession contracts are for a limited period—usually 15–30 years, depending on the context and sector. Finally, the government, as owner of the assets, retains much closer involvement and oversight in concessions.

These differences have a number of implications, but perhaps the most important is that the concessionaire's only asset is the right to revenue— the cash flow—from customers for the life of the concession. Moreover, that asset's value is uncertain because of natural variations in demand and tariffs and because of the possibility of early contract termination by the government. (Nearly every concession contract contains a clause granting the government the right to cancel the concession under certain conditions, with or without some agreement on compensation for such action.) But that revenue is the only asset an operator can pledge against a loan: no land, plants, or machinery can be pledged because all physical assets remain state property. In the event of early contract termination, lenders often have no rights to revenue generated during the remainder of the original concession. These shortcomings, intrinsic to concessions, increase risks, raise capital costs, and affect financing terms.

For financing BOT projects, another issue can also affect the cost of capital: the single-buyer risk. Any debt will usually be secured against the value of the contract to supply the services, not against the assets of the contractor. Thus, the appraisal of the project's credit risk will depend primarily on whether the ultimate purchaser is creditworthy and on the contractual arrangements for guaranteeing payment. A variety of arrangements to mitigate this risk can and have been used, for example, escrow accounts for a portion of revenues for services. None of these arrangements can get around the difficulties of dealing with a nearly insolvent utility whose tariffs are too low or which is dramatically inefficient. And indeed the experience in Mexico with BOT in the water sector has seen a number of such type of problems. In such cases, the government owns that company that will be the ultimate borrower (via guarantee or other provisions), in which case the BOT contract is no more than a combination of a government-guaranteed loan with a performance contract. This arrangement will not solve the problems faced by governments that are not creditworthy and unable to finance investments in extending infrastructure service.

Benefits of Concessions

Concessions of (quasi) natural monopolies offer several advantages. First, they allow private participation in sectors in which private ownership is constitutionally, legally, or politically untenable. Second, if awarded competitively (which tends to be the case), concessions enable competition for the market (as opposed to competition in the market) and ought to dissipate monopoly rents—ensuring the most efficient operator and, in principle, facilitating regulatory oversight. Third, concessions can encourage cost efficiency, particularly when granted under price-cap regulation or rate-of-return regulation if cost referential benchmarks are used. Under price-cap regulation, concession contracts specify maximum prices for set quantities of goods or services, permitting cost savings to accrue to the concessionaire, at least between tariff reviews. Finally, concessions can achieve optimal pricing even when sunk costs rule out contestability, because competition occurs before firms commit to investment programs.

Drawbacks of Concessions

Disadvantages of concessions include the need for complex design and monitoring systems when multiple targets are involved, the inability to cover every conceivable contingency, the difficulty in enforcing contracts (and limiting incentives to renegotiate), the need to account for poor service quality, and the lack of investment incentives toward the end of the concession period because of the fixed-term nature of contracts and the inability to commit to price adjustments over the life of the concession. Government's inability to be credible in its commitment to no renegotiation creates opportunities to use and abuse renegotiation, raising doubts about the initial price bid on which a concession is awarded (Mueller 2001; Spiller 1993).

Incentives for concessionaires to maintain transferred assets properly can be strengthened by compensating them at the end of the concession period with an amount linked to the winning bid for the next concession period or to investments not yet depreciated. Bidding for concessions remains an attractive approach if properly designed—and if abuses after the award are contained, enforcement is appropriate, and (especially) if repeated bidding is practical.

Concession and Regulatory Design

Effective sector performance is driven by proper concession and regulatory design, and both are somehow intertwined. "Concession design" means the award process, the award criteria, prequalification requirements, ownership restrictions, labor force adjustment issues, investment obligations versus output targets, guarantees, concession length, termination clauses and compensation rules, contingency clauses, performance bonds, conflict resolution mechanisms and appeals structure, allocation of risks, and so forth. Regulatory framework means choice of regulatory regime (rate of return versus price cap), tariff structure, adjustment of tariff procedures and triggers, ordinary and extraordinary tariff reviews, valuation of assets, cost allocation, asset base, quality of service standards, informational requirements, regulatory accounting, regulatory instruments, penalties and fees, consumer rights, services to be regulated, and all that has to do with the structure, organization, and procedures with the regulatory agency. Both are related, and indeed some gray areas exist where the concept could be considered part of the concession design or part of the regulatory framework.

3

Concessions and the Problem of Renegotiation

Over the past 15 years concessions have significantly improved infrastructure services in many countries. Still, privately provided services have raised many concerns. In some cases conflicts have emerged because operators have not complied with contract clauses, have charged tariffs considered excessive, or have been unresponsive to users. In other cases governments have not honored contract clauses to adjust or index prices. In still other cases concessions have been abandoned by private operators or taken over by governments as a result of operator bankruptcies.

But perhaps the biggest problem with concessions has been the high incidence of contract renegotiation shortly after their award—often undermining the competitive auction allocation process, consumer welfare, and sector performance; increasing public opposition to private participation in infrastructure; and compromising the credibility of the reform program. Moreover the significant cost of the renegotiation process incurred by both parties can induce large dead-weight welfare losses. If concessions are renegotiated shortly after their award, as often happens, the initial bidding or auction turns into a bilateral negotiation between the winning operator and the government—undermining competitive discipline of the auction. At that stage the operator has significant leverage, because the government is often unable to reject renegotiation and is usually unwilling to claim failure—and let the operator abandon the concession—for fear of political backlash and additional transaction costs. In such cases the operator, through renegotiations, can undermine all the benefits of the bidding- or auction-led competitive process.

Renegotiation Incidence and Incidents

Renegotiation occurs when the original contract and financial impact of a concession contract is significantly altered and such changes were not the result of contingencies spelled out in the contract. For example, stated and standard tariff adjustments resulting from inflation or other stated drivers do not count as renegotiation. Nor do periodic tariff reviews stipulated in a contract, or contingencies (such as significant devaluations) in a contract that induces tariff changes. Only when substantial departures from the original contract occurred and the contract is amended can one say that a renegotiation took place.

Excluding the telecommunications sector (which is far less subject to renegotiation, mostly because of the sector's higher competitiveness and availability of potential new entrants, and which was privatized rather than concessioned), more than 41 percent of infrastructure concessions in Latin America and the Caribbean have been renegotiated. The hardest hit sectors have been the transportation sector and the water and sanitation sector with renegotiation incidence of 55 and 75 percent, respectively. Of additional concern has been the very fast timing for renegotiation. The time between the start of operations and the renegotiation of contracts has averaged about 2 years, despite original contract agreements of 20–30 years. Moreover, this estimated incidence of renegotiation is likely an underestimate because the process is ongoing, and in the next few years additional concessions will likely be renegotiated.

In principle, renegotiation can be a positive instrument when it addresses the inherently incomplete nature of concession contracts. Properly used, renegotiation can enhance welfare. Although some renegotiation is desirable, appropriate, and to be expected, this high incidence exceeds expected and reasonable levels and raises concerns about the validity of the concession model. It might even indicate excessively opportunistic behavior by new operators or by governments. Such behavior undermined the efficiency of the process and the overall welfare, because renegotiation takes place between government and the operator only, so it is not subject to competitive pressures and their associated discipline. When used opportunistically or strategically by an operator or government, to secure additional benefits, and not driven by the incompleteness of a contract, renegotiation can undermine the integrity of a concession and reduce welfare and threaten the desired structural reform program in infrastructure. The high incidence of negotiation reported here should indeed be a cause of concern.

Renegotiation, particularly opportunistic renegotiation, can reduce or eliminate the expected benefits of competitive bidding. If the auction is designed well and provides adequate incentives, competitive bidding for the right to operate a concession for a given number of years should elicit the most efficient operator. If bidders believe that renegotiation is feasible and likely, however, their strategic behavior and their bids will be effected, and the process will not be likely to select the most efficient operator as intended.

In such an environment two elements play major roles in determining the bids of operators, aside from how efficient they are in providing the service and what information they have about the concession. The first element is the operators' assessment of the likelihood of renegotiation; the second is the operators' assessment of their own ability to renegotiate. If both assessments are positive, operators bid to secure a concession. Then, if they win the contract, they request a renegotiation with the government to secure better terms. This approach distorts the competitive process, because the winning operator may be the one most skilled in renegotiation or the one most optimistic about its likelihood, rather than the one most efficient— particularly if the government cannot credibly commit to a policy of no renegotiation—as it is intended.

Finally another adverse factor of renegotiations is the added costs and dead-weight welfare losses it induces. The process of renegotiations can be fairly long and costly on both sides, that of the operator and that of the regulator or government. It requires a fair amount of information gathering and analysis and the running of costs and financial models. It often lasts three to twelve months and can tie up the regulator's limited resources—human and otherwise—for that entire period, at the expense of the other tasks and operations the regulator is responsible for. For renegotiations in which a clear welfare benefit is evident, the tradeoffs might be warranted, but for opportunistic ones—aiming at best, at redistribution of resources—the impact of those costs and locking those resources can be quite damaging.

The Principle of Financial Equilibrium in Regulated Markets: More Regulation, More Renegotiation

Almost by definition, certain features of regulated sectors make them more prone to renegotiation. First, regulation constrains the actions that a concessionaire can take, the most important being the setting of tariffs. Second, tariffs are expected to be set so that they allow the concessionaire to earn reasonable profits. When firms are not able to earn expected returns, they expect, logically enough, a change in contract terms. This premise is behind the so-called financial equilibrium clause implicit or explicit in most concession service contracts and legislation. That clause is, in principle, a valid pillar of any concession contract, because private investors should be allowed to earn a fair rate of return on their investments. Nevertheless, the financial equilibrium also ought to be subject to a number of provisos, including a conditioning to cost-efficient operation. Yet the costs of providing services are rarely linked to a benchmark of efficient operations, and when they are, such costs are often disputed.

The following equation offers a simplified representation of financial equilibrium, where revenues minus costs should provide the appropriate return on investment:

$$R = PQ - OC - T - D = rKi,$$

where R is profits, P is prices or tariffs, Q is quantity or output, OC is operation and maintenance costs, T is taxes, D is depreciation, r is the opportunity cost of capital, and Ki is invested capital. If the award criterion is a transfer fee, it appears under Ki. If it is the lowest tariff, it appears under P. In principle, any appropriate bid, whether based on K or P, has behind it an analysis that balances this equation.

A strategic or opportunistic bid is, presumably, one in which the left-hand side of the equation (profits) is less than the right-hand side (returns to capital). Here strategic, opportunistic, or aggressive bidding refers to bids that do not provide firms with financial equilibrium—that is, the costs of submitted bids exceed revenues. That is, bidding a transfer fee or a tariff such that

$$R = PQ - OC - T - D < rKi.$$

The objective of such a bid is to win the concession with the expectation of later renegotiation—arguing that the equation does not balance, and higher tariffs or lower future investments are needed to restore financial equilibrium.

Ample anecdotal evidence indicates the existence of low-ball bidding on concessions, and that should raise a red flag. Examples from Latin American countries include an airport concession in which the winning bidder promised to deliver nearly half of revenue to the government and invest more than US$1 billion, a bid to construct a new toll road that was to be transferred to the government (and thus would have the investment fully amortized) in less than seven years, bids that had transfer fees more than three times (and in some cases 10 times) those from other bidders, bids that promised significant tariff cuts and significant investment, and so on.

Strategic underbidding (or overbidding, depending on award criteria), to some extent encouraged by the incompleteness of contracts, also may explain the high proportion of renegotiation. As noted, many firms have won concession contracts by strategically underbidding (or overbidding), with the expectation that they would be able to renegotiate in the future, and governments have often been unable to commit to enforcing these agreements. If all potential bidders account for that possibility, an auction could still elicit the most efficient operator—but with significant underbids or overbids. That argument has two problems, however. First, because renegotiation is a bilateral negotiation, the final outcome need not be guided by efficiency and welfare concerns, and rents could be transferred. Second, although any potential operator could submit a bid with the expectation of renegotiation, expectations might vary among bidders and not necessarily be correlated with their efficiency. Moreover, some enterprises may possess a systematic advantage in renegotiation and so be more likely to win a concession through underbidding (or overbidding). As a result a firm with high affiliation and high costs could win an auction.

Guasch, Kartacheva, and Quesada (2000) develop this framework and show the equilibrium strategy to be of that nature. With the other competitors gone, renegotiation then occurs in a noncompetitive atmosphere, and the operator and the government engage in bilateral renegotiation. In such negotiations governments are often in a disadvantaged position that grants significant leverage to the operators, enabling the operators to improve their positions (capture more rents) relative to their original bids.

Bidding, Renegotiation, and Government Responses: Sanctity of the Bid

In a regulated environment where firms are not free to adjust prices however they see fit, and in the event of adverse economic conditions that do not allow them to earn expected returns, expecting a change in contract terms to restore profitability—that is, renegotiation—is rational. Thus firms seeking concession rights might logically submit their most optimistic bids, with the expectation that if things do not turn out well they can renegotiate the terms of the contract, drawing on the financial equilibrium clause. But what if a firm submits an unreasonable bid, one that has a very high transfer fee or very low tariff, and then, as expected, the financial equation does not hold? Should the firm be held accountable to its bid, or should the firm be bailed out?

The right answer is that, barring major external factors, operators should be held accountable to their bids, and if petitions for renegotiation are turned down, operators ought to feel free to abandon the projects, if they choose to do so (with the corresponding penalties). The appropriate behavior for government is to uphold the sanctity of the bid and not concede to opportunistic requests for renegotiation. Doing so may lead to the abandonment of a concession, but that is a price worth paying and, in fact, can help government establish a reputation of not being easy in terms of renegotiation demands and, in doing so, would discourage future aggressive bids.

What should be done more often is for governments to reject opportunistic requests for renegotiation and, in such cases, allow concessions to fail. Such outcomes would reduce the incidence of renegotiation. That is a key issue in private concessions of infrastructure services—yet one that is often resolved in favor of operators. Thus aggressive bidding and the high incidence of renegotiation should not be surprising.

But governments have had a hard time adopting that strategy, because accepting concession failures brings political costs. Yet, although cancellations and renationalizations of private infrastructure projects attract headlines, they have been relatively uncommon. Of the 2,485 private infrastructure projects concluded in 1990–2001, just 48—less than 2 percent—saw the exit of the private sector (box 3.1). Such data, however, may simply indicate that governments have been unable to commit to a policy of no renegotiation and have conceded to opportunistic renegotiation.

Many governments have conceded rents to operators during opportunistic renegotiations when it would have been more appropriate to hold

---

Box 3.1 *An Overview of Canceled Private Infrastructure Projects*

Worldwide, out of a total of 2,485 projects granted in 1990–2001, 48 private infrastructure projects were canceled with total investment commitments of US$19.8 billion. Of these, 19 were toll roads (all in Mexico), 9 were energy projects (all but 1 in electricity), 7 were water and sanitation projects, 8 were telecommunications projects, and the rest were in transportation sectors other than toll roads. The highest incidence of cancellation by sector occurred in toll roads, where 5.8 percent of projects were canceled, and water and sanitation, where 3.5 percent of projects saw the exit of the private sector.

Source: Harris (2002).

the operators to their initial bids—even though in the short term, before a government establishes a reputation for not conceding to opportunistic renegotiation, such an approach would increase the number of abandoned concessions. Thus it could be argued that the incidence of abandoned concessions has perhaps not been high enough to establish a needed reputation signaling a credible commitment to a policy of no opportunistic renegotiation and thus to reach the steady-state "good" equilibrium of much limited renegotiation demand and incidence.

A second best, but difficult, approach for government is to reject aggressive bids. But that is seldom done. Indeed, such bids are celebrated as a sign that government has secured a very high transfer fee or very low tariff. Paradoxically, even well-meaning governments might avoid disqualifying aggressive offers for fear of being accused of corruption or favoritism. For example, for a water concession in a Latin American country, the best offer had a transfer fee that was several times the second best offer. Yet even though the bidding documents allowed the government to disqualify highly aggressive offers, for the reasons just explained, the government accepted the best offer. Shortly after the contract was awarded, the operator requested a renegotiation—and eventually the concession was abandoned.

Given that renegotiation requests are often accepted and resolved in favor of concessionaires, aggressive bidding and frequent renegotiation demands should not be surprising Thus submitting their most optimistic bids for concessions, with the expectation that if things do not turn out well, they will be able to renegotiate the terms of the contract, often makes sense for firms. Financial equilibrium imbalance, however, can be claimed, and usually is, at any time and independent of having submitted a financially nonviable bid. The informational asymmetries on costs makes properly evaluating those requests difficult for governments and creates incentives for firms to argue financial imbalance.

The Case of Directly Adjudicated Concessions

One interesting empirical regularity from the data collected provides additional support to the rent-seeking thesis: the low incidence of renegotiation—about 8 percent—on concessions granted not through competitive bidding but through direct adjudication or bilateral negotiation between the government and a single operator, as a result of government invitation or operator request. A plausible explanation for that low renegotiation incidence is that any rents to be captured were secured through the initial bilateral negotiation, reducing or eliminating the need for opportunistic operator behavior after the concession is awarded. Moreover, the lack of competition might rule out questionable (that is, financially unsustainable) bids.

In direct adjudication of concession, any renegotiation usually comes from a new administration, questioning a "sweet" deal granted by the previous administration, or from the same administration with different priorities. Examples include power purchase agreements with independent power producers in various countries and road concessions in a couple countries.

The lower incidence of renegotiation in directly adjudicated concessions should not be interpreted as an endorsement of that process. To the contrary, it shows the problems with that process—rent capture, opportunities for corruption—and indicates that it should not be used. Government-led renegotiation also raises questions about competition.[1] Operators can account for the risk of renegotiation in their bids, again possibly leading to the selection not of the most efficient operator, but the one best able to bear the risk. The result will be a contaminated process that has higher regulatory risk, translating into higher capital costs and higher tariffs. Thus government-led can be as damaging as operator-led renegotiation.

Other Drivers of Renegotiation

Governments also hold some blame for many problems with concessions. Governments have often behaved opportunistically and interfered with contract clauses—forcing renegotiation, cutting tariffs unilaterally, not authorizing tariff increases allowed in the contract, and so on. Indeed, nearly 30 percent of renegotiations are initiated by governments. While some of the renegotiations might be desirable, from a welfare standpoint, if not driven by contingencies expressed in the contract, such actions can damage the institutionality and credibility of the process. Although envisioning the eradication of government influence on regulatory decisions is hard, properly designed concessions and regulations should deter such behavior.

Poor concession design riddled with ambiguities also opens the doors for renegotiation demands. The reasons for poor concession designs have

---

1. Relative to direct adjudication, concessions awarded through competitive bidding entail systematic cost reductions of more than 20 percent (Dornberger, Meadowcroft, and Thompson 1986).

varied from political cycles to pure carelessness to misaligned incentives to lack of understanding of key determinants, and perhaps driven by vested interests so as to open possibilities for capturing supranormal rents. Political constraints could be viewed as time constraints: the desire to accomplish too much in too little time (the duration of the administration). In many Latin American countries (Argentina, Brazil, Mexico, and Peru) at the start of the process, constitutions forbade immediate reelection of sitting presidents.[2] Thus concessions were often awarded hastily.

The clustering of concession awards within a few years supports that hypothesis. Reform governments have feared that they had limited windows of opportunity to make their policy changes irreversible and so have awarded concessions in a number of sectors almost simultaneously without taking sufficient time to design the contracts appropriately and to set and implement appropriate regulatory frameworks. Some efforts have emphasized speed, leaving aside acquisition of information about markets and specification of contingencies in contracts. Such shortcomings and contracts that were not watertight add to the incompleteness of contracts and increase opportunities for renegotiation.

In addition the intrinsic informational asymmetries on costs between the operator and the regulator provide incentives for opportunistic demands for renegotiation. Even if the bid is proper and not opportunistic in the sense described above, down the road, operators can claim cost increases, driven by a number of factors, that unbalance their financial equilibrium and thus request increases in tariffs to restore that equilibrium. The anchor of all those claims is the usual clause of financial equilibrium in concession contracts. Thus describing in the contract the context and applicability of that clause—with specific contingencies as much as possible—is of foremost importance and should not be used to allow just any cost increases or demand decreases to justify a tariff increase request. If the environment is conducive to renegotiation, those requests are bound to proliferate with all their added costs and implications.

Finally, macroeconomic shocks also bear some of the blame for renegotiation. Exchange rate risk is a major factor because project revenue is usually denominated in local currency, and financing is usually in foreign

---

2. Yet in three of those countries—Argentina, Brazil, and Peru—late in their elected periods governments were able to pass constitutional amendments that permitted immediate reelection and the three presidents were elected for second terms.

currency. Such problems occurred in Mexico in 1994–95, in Brazil in the late 1990s, and especially in Argentina in late 2001, where devaluation led to major problems and renegotiations in almost all of the country's concessions. Although operators and in some cases governments can do little to prevent such shocks, clear contract guidelines should indicate what level of changes triggers an adjustment and how to proceed and renegotiate under such conditions. Those guidelines, along with the use of existing financial hedging instruments, can provide some comfort and decrease regulatory risk for investors (Guasch 2003).

4

Anecdotal Evidence of the Drivers of Renegotiation

In the broad sense, problems with concessions occur when efficient performance—as reflected in service costs, access, quality, and operator returns—is undermined by poor decisions and actions at the design stage or after the contract award. Poor decisions, ambiguities, and actions at the design stage can lead to unnecessarily high tariffs or set the stage for conflicts down the road. Poor decisions and actions after the contract award are problematic when they improve (or worsen) the financial terms for the operator over the terms agreed upon at the bidding stage, through bilateral renegotiation between the winner operator and the government.

In addition, improper regulatory framework and poor regulatory oversight increases the chances of conflict, rent capture by operators (situation that translates into higher tariffs than appropriate), or opportunistic behavior by government, and all these changes facilitate renegotiation. Both elements increase undesirable uncertainty about the stability of the agreed-upon contractual terms or rules of the game. Finally, external shocks, although an exogenous factor, can also significantly affect the financial equilibrium of a concession and usually (correctly) induce renegotiation. The consequences of all these issues range from worse sector performance than is desirable to abandonment of the concession by the operator, both of which cause increased dissatisfaction among users and potentially lead to rejection of reforms.

Most problems with concessions are caused by the following:

- Inadequate attention to political and institutional issues
- Government tolerance of aggressive bidding and the problems that it causes

- Faulty contract designs
- Governments not honoring contract clauses, forcing renegotiation, and changing the rules and effects of a concession
- Defective regulation and its effects
- Macroeconomic shocks (although these are external factors).

Political and Institutional Issues

Problems often arise at the very beginning, when public enterprises are chosen for concession programs. Because of unresolved conflicts, some concessions are never awarded, and others never start operations. Such problems are typically driven by a harried process and by insufficient efforts to seek consensus and support from critical stakeholders—such as enterprise employees opposed to a concession for fear of job losses or some users opposed for fear of tariff increases.

That conflict led to the cancellation of telecommunications concessions in Colombia and Uruguay and of electricity distribution concessions in Arequipa, Peru, and has considerably delayed private participation in ports in most countries in Latin America and the Caribbean. Inadequate attention to political and institutional issues has also led to the abandonment of many concessions in the Philippines, including an airport radar contract, a power plant contract, and a highway contract. Among the problems in these concessions were unresolved turf battles and unclear jurisdiction among government agencies, poorly defined technological and other terms in concession contracts (leading to contract cancellation or renegotiation), and political capture of contracts to benefit domestic over foreign concessionaires.

Aggressive Bidding

Aggressive bidding often means that, from the start, concession operations are not financially viable. As noted, firms may consider aggressive bidding a rational strategy if governments are unable to commit to a policy of no renegotiation. Firms are then likely to submit unsustainable bids with the intention of renegotiating better terms after the concession has been awarded. If such renegotiation is not allowed, abandonment of the concession often follows—and if it is allowed, the benefits of competitive bidding are undermined. Two examples of each outcome follow.

Abandoned Concessions

The following two examples are typical of aggressive bids where the government did not agree to the operators' contract renegotiation demands, and as result the operators abandoned the concessions, which were taken over by the countries' governments.

WATER SERVICES IN BUENOS AIRES. In May 1999 the province of Buenos Aires (Argentina) used competitive bidding to award a concession for the private provision of water services. Of the seven firms that prequalified for the operation, four submitted bids. The award criterion was the highest (lump-sum) transfer fee to the government of the province. The winning bidder, Azurix, offered US$277 million for the right to provide water services in three zones of the province. The concession contract also required Azurix to invest US$500 million in improvements and service extensions in the first five years of the concession. The other firms bid US$15 million, US$10 million and US$8 million, respectively, to provide the same service.

Although the significant differences among the offers raised eyebrows, the provincial government awarded the concession to Azurix, claiming significant success. Yet problems began shortly afterward, when Azurix sought to renegotiate the contract. Among other conflicts, Azurix and the government accused each other of noncompliance with agreed-upon terms. The government did not concede to a renegotiation, however—one of the few cases where that has happened around the world. As of result, in 2002 Azurix abandoned the concession, and the government reassumed responsibility for providing water services. The case was left in the hands of the courts, with Azurix seeking to secure compensation for its costs and investments in the concession.

This case shows the problems that often result from aggressive bidding. Although other water providers questioned the financial viability of the Azurix offer, the government did not perform or request a more detailed analysis of the winning bid. The government did, however, hold Azurix accountable for its bid.

ELECTRICITY DISTRIBUTION IN CENTRAL AND NORTHERN PERU. In late 1998, after four years of success with the privatization of the electricity distribution companies serving Lima, arrangements were made for four regional distribution companies serving central and northern Peru to be partially sold to the private sector. Although only 30 percent of the companies' assets were to be transferred initially, all of their remaining assets were expected to be privatized in two subsequent phases. In the second phase, after three years of operation, the acquiring company was required to buy another 30 percent of the assets at the same price as in the initial bidding. Also 10 percent of assets were reserved for company workers and the other 30 percent were to be put on the stock market to be acquired by the general public. This last feature was standard practice in all the other power sector privatizations in Peru.

This contract had the same characteristics as Peru's other electricity distribution contracts, with one important difference: the explicit condition that the acquiring party would have total management control from the beginning even though it initially controlled only 30 percent of voting rights. Moreover, operators were allowed to bid for any of the distribution companies individually or for all of them jointly. The bids offered by the winning party are shown in table 4.1.

Two other companies offered bids that were about half the winning bid for all four companies. At the time of the bidding, distribution tariffs for the four electricity companies were known, including the acquired assets replacement value—the investment part of the tariff. (Peru's distribution tariffs are based on forward-looking costs for a model efficient company.) The asset replacement value was about US$240 million, half the amount offered for the companies. Although the companies' assets included some subtransmission and other facilities, the winning bid for the distribution business was well above what could be expected to be recovered through tariffs. (The remaining part of the tariffs cover operation and maintenance, administration, and other operating costs, also based on a model efficient company.)

In November 2001 the regulator approved a new asset replacement value and distribution tariffs. During the tariff resetting process, the company insisted that the assets were valued based on what it paid in the privatization, not on established criteria for valuing assets. The regulator did not accept this argument. At the end of 2001, when the obligation to buy the second 30 percent of shares kicked in, the company refused to proceed and sued the government for breach of contract. The winning operator ultimately abandoned the concession after it failed to find a partner willing to provide the money for the additional 30 percent of shares at the agreed-upon price.

In March 2002 the government regained control of the distribution companies. This chain of events is an example of an aggressive bid in which the government or regulator refused to concede to operator demands for renegotiation.

Renegotiated Concessions

The following two examples illustrate common renegotiation demands by operators accommodated by the government after questionable aggressive bids.

Table 4.1 *Winning Bids for Four Electricity Distribution Companies in Central and Northern Peru, 1998*

Company	Cost of 30% of shares (thousands of US$)	Equivalent cost of 100% of shares (thousands of US$)	Number of consumers	Cost per consumer (US$)
Electrocentro	32,690	108,967	249,531	437
Electronoroeste	22,885	76,283	161,685	472
Electronorte	22,119	73,730	141,497	521
Hidrandina	67,879	226,263	286,190	791
Total	145,573	485,243	838,903	578

Source: Author's compilation.

AIRPORT CONCESSION IN LIMA. In early 2001 Lima's airport was concessioned to a consortium, led by Frankfurt Airport operator, Bechtel, and a local partner, that submitted the highest bid. The criterion was the percentage of gross revenue that the operator would commit to turn over to the state. The winning bid offered the state 47 percent of gross revenue in addition to a commitment to invest more than US$1 billion and construct a second landing strip by the 11th year of the 30-year concession.

Although that appears to be a very attractive bid from the government's perspective and as such was lauded, it also appears financially questionable. It means that from the residual 53 percent of gross revenue, the operator will be able to cover operating costs, amortize investments, and earn a fair rate of return on investments. Shortly after the award, the winning consortium began asking to renegotiate the contract. The operator has been delaying agreed-upon investments, and the bickering from both sides has been a constant. The concession contract was renegotiated at the end of 2003, adjusting investment obligations and the percentage of the gross revenues to be given to the state each year.

RAILWAY PRIVATIZATION IN MEXICO. In 1996 the Mexican government auctioned the Northeast Railway line as part of its previously announced plan to privatize the Mexican National Railways. The winning bidder, a consortium of Kansas City Southern and Transportes Maritimos Mexicanas, offered US$1.5 billion for the 80 percent stake in the line being auctioned—three times the next highest bidder. This gap led to speculation that the winners had bid too much, and their share prices dropped.

Shortly afterward, their financial backers pulled out, and the consortium was forced to recognize that it could not finance the deal. The consortium then sought to renegotiate the bid. The government accepted this proposition, and under the renegotiated deal the consortium bought a 55 percent share for US$700 million, Mexican National Railways retained a 25 percent share, and the Secretaria de Comunicaciones y Transportes retained (as originally planned) the remaining 20 percent. This renegotiation was done without reopening the bidding process, in absolute secrecy from the other bidders, and is an example of a process lacking transparency and a government complying with an inappropriate renegotiation request.

Faulty Contract Designs

Faulty contract designs encompass the design elements of concessions (box 4.1). Faulty designs include questionable objectives, such as trying to secure a maximum transfer fee rather than achieve sector efficiency. This situation can occur when excessive exclusivity rights are granted—as in Jamaica's sale of its telecommunications company, when the winning bidder was given a 25-year monopoly and a guaranteed 18 percent annual return. Faulty designs also include excessively generous terms, as with a number of power purchase agreements with independent power producers—in the Dominican Republic and elsewhere—that have led to unnecessarily high tariffs and poor services.

Faulty designs can also involve the use of inadequate award criteria, direct adjudication, or minimum prices or tariffs. Another common source of conflict that often leads to renegotiation involves requests for investment commitments in contracts, usually because questions are raised about the realized levels and true market value of those investments. Ambiguous terms, such as on guidelines for adjusting tariffs during periodic review, can also lead to conflicts and renegotiation.

In addition, many issues that might not endanger concessions can make them more onerous or costly for users, such as allowing significant management fees or not requiring the use of market prices when purchasing equipment. Some telecommunications firms in Latin America and the Caribbean have secured management fees equal to nearly half their annual profits. In other cases firms have been able to buy equipment from subsidiaries at inflated prices.

Faulty designs can also be caused by improper regulatory oversight. The impacts of faulty designs vary considerably: they can lead to renegotiation, abandonment of a concession, or other unappealing outcomes. They

Box 4.1 *Common Mistakes in Concessions in Latin American and Caribbean Countries*

An excessive number of concessions have encountered problems, leading to contract renegotiations and undermining the credibility of the process. Although some renegotiations are efficient and necessary, many are opportunistic and should be deterred. The most common mistakes made in concessions are described below.

Preconcession issues

- Disregard for political economy; governments not seeking potential supporters and not articulating the motivation and objectives for the concession. (Examples: electricity distribution in Argentina and Peru; water in Cochabamba, Bolivia; telecommunications in Paraguay.)
- Not accounting for labor rationalization issues. If workers are not involved and plans are not made to deal with and compensate them, the concession will likely fail. (Examples: telecommunications in Colombia and Uruguay, ports in Brazil.)
- Improper sector or firm restructuring prior to the concession. The best time to reshape market structure (horizontally and vertically), facilitate competition, and improve regulation is before the concession. (Examples: electricity in Brazil and Chile, telecommunications in most countries.)
- Failure to adjust tariffs before the award or failure to set a schedule for doing so in the contract. (Examples: telecommunications in Argentina, Peru, and the Republica Bolivariana de Venezúela.)
- Excessively optimistic government demand forecasts. (Examples: toll roads in Argentina, Brazil, Colombia, and Mexico.)

Concession design issues

- Inadequate prequalification screening. (Examples: toll roads in Colombia, telecommunications in Guatemala, railways in Mexico.)
- Using means rather than outcomes as requirements for operators. (Examples: water in Buenos Aires, Argentina, and in most sectors in Bolivia; ports in Peru.)
- Ambiguous conflict resolution procedures. (Example: water in Brazil, tollroads in Colombia.)
- Vague or inappropriate terms for the end of the concession. (Examples: almost all cases.)
- Inappropriate management of risks. (Examples: most cases.)

(Box continues on the following page.)

Box 4.1 (continued)

- Improper use of guarantees. (Examples: airport landing strip in Colombia, roads in the Dominican Republic, toll roads in Mexico.)
- Not accounting for universal service obligations.
- Inadequate and poor use of performance obligation penalties.
- Misalignment of incentives between adviser or investment banks and concession objectives. (Example: telecommunications in Jamaica.)
- Changing contract terms after issuing the call for bids. (Examples: telecommunications in Argentina and Nicaragua; ports in Peru.)
- Not providing incentives to expand a network (when a standalone network has been concessioned). The most common cases have involved electricity transmission and railway track. (Examples: electricity in Argentina, Brazil, and Peru; railways in Argentina, Bolivia, Mexico, and Peru.)

Concession award issues

- Use of direct adjudication rather than competitive bidding. (Examples: power purchase agreements in the Dominican Republic, Guatemala, and Honduras; toll roads in the Dominican Republic.)
- Multiple award criteria, which can lead to wasteful rent seeking and opportunities for corruption and arbitrary selection of winners. Multiple criteria can also lead to lawsuits by losers, paralyzing the concession. (Examples: telecommunications in Guatemala; airports in Costa Rica; railroads in Argentina.)
- Questionable single criteria. (Examples: toll roads in Mexico, which were awarded based on the shortest proposed operating period; water services in Argentina and Manila, the Philippines, which were awarded based on the largest tariff discount.)
- Use of single lump-sum transfer to government rather than annual payments or a lump sum disbursed in annual installments. (Examples: most countries.)
- Choosing fiscal objectives rather than (long-term) efficiency objectives. (Examples: telecommunications in Jamaica, Turks and Caicos Islands, and the Republica Bolivariana de Venezúela.)

Regulatory issues

- Absence of regulatory and sector legal framework prior to concession. (Examples: telecommunications in Argentina, Trinidad and Tobago, and

Turks and Caicos Islands; electricity in Brazil and the Dominican Republic; water in Bolivia; toll roads in Chile and Mexico.)
- Disregard for institutional development. (Examples: most countries.)
- Lack of independent regulators. (Examples: all sectors in Mexico; telecommunications and transportation in Argentina; electricity in the Dominican Republic; water and electricity in Brazil.)
- Excessive regulator discretion. (Example: electricity in Nicaragua.)
- Excessive political composition (including politicians, user groups, and operators) of regulatory commissions. (Examples: telecommunications in Peru; water in Argentina and Brazil.)
- Failure to single out competitive segments of the sector and limit regulation to noncompetitive segments.
- Inappropriate setting of initial prices when using price-cap regulation. (Examples: electricity in Turks and Caicos Islands.)
- Vague network access clauses, undermining liberalization and competition. (Examples: almost all cases.)
- Failure to account for dynamic and static efficiency in choice and mode of regulation. (Examples: water in most countries.)
- Inappropriate or excessive exclusivity rights. (Examples: telecommunications in Jamaica, Turks and Caicos Islands, and the Republica Bolivariana de Venezúela.)
- Inability to make a credible commitment to no frivolous renegotiation, or providing excessive opportunities for renegotiation. This issue is complex, and most countries have been unable to avoid it. (Examples: railways and roads in Argentina and Mexico; airports in Peru.)
- Failure to include strong information requirements to operators—to provide needed information to the regulator—in concession contracts; such requirements are essential to effective regulation. (Examples: telecommunications in Peru and Turks and Caicos Islands; water in Argentina and Chile.)
- Failure to impose proper accounting standards on regulated firms, which undermines cost assessments required to align tariffs with costs. (Examples: most countries.)
- Undefined jurisdiction between antitrust and regulatory agencies to oversee operator actions. (Examples: most countries.)
- Absence of technical training for regulators and absence of improvements in administrative capacity. (Examples: most countries.)
- Failure to hold operators accountable for their bids—the sanctity of bid issue. (Examples: most countries.)

also affect sector performance by not allowing, delaying, or reducing efficiency and improvements that were expected or promised when reforms were sold to the public. Popular dissatisfaction can end or even reverse private participation in infrastructure. The following examples illustrate some of these problems.

Poor Design, a Hurried Pace, and Financial Disaster: Renegotiation in Mexico's Highway Program

In 1997 the Mexican government announced that it would spend US$3.3 billion over the next 30 years to restructure the financing of 52 highways built under private concessions of toll roads in the early 1990s. This renegotiation and bailout of private operators followed a program riddled with design problems. The first was that concessions were awarded to the operators that submitted the shortest time to operate each concession—a questionable criterion by any economic principle.

The second problem was that the government provided extremely optimistic guarantees of traffic volumes, implicit insurance for construction cost overruns, and a state-run banking sector that provided loans without detailed analysis of the structure and sustainability of the projects being financed.[1] Finally, the hurried pace of the program led to incomplete designs and specifications for road construction, and rushed engineering studies and hasty cost projections created ample opportunity for padding budgets. The resulting bids covered very short concession periods (with most running 6–12 years, although one bid was for just 18 months!), caused significant cost overruns, required high tolls to support the short concession periods, and—as should have been anticipated—culminated in economic and financial disaster. Mexico's 1994 financial crisis accelerated the problem. The government had to retake nearly 80 percent of the concessions at an estimated cost of US$7 billion to US$12 billion. In addition, questions have been raised about the transparency of the program.

---

1. Excessively optimistic traffic forecasts have been common in highway concessions, mostly to make the concession more attractive to private investors. In Mexico, on average, traffic was 60 percent lower than predicted, and in Colombia, 40 percent lower. Also cost overuns have been quite common and often guaranteed. For example, in Colombia costs were 40 percent higher than contracted values, mostly because of higher expropriation costs, design changes, and inclusion of additional features.

Renegotiation of a Water and Sanitation Concession in the City of Buenos Aires

In Argentina the responsibility for water and sanitation services was decentralized to provinces in 1980, but the central government retained control over these services in the capital. In 1993, water and sanitation services in Buenos Aires were concessioned through competitive bidding to the private sector. The main objective of the concession was to expand water and sanitation services in the absence of adequate public financial resources: in a city of 9 million residents, half lacked one or both services.

The concessionaire was selected in two phases. First, five firms were prequalified to bid based on their technical, administrative, and financial capacity. A price competition followed in which a baseline tariff was specified and the contenders submitted a price bid as a percentage (above or below) of the baseline tariff. Aguas Argentinas (a consortium of domestic and foreign entities) won the price competition with a bid that was to reduce average tariffs by 27 percent. The Argentine government ultimately decided to forgo compensation for the rights to use existing facilities. The value of these use rights was not trivial: the water company was operating with positive cash flows and earning a positive return on its assets. The expectation was that competitive bidding would transfer those rents to users and that the subsidy could be justified because of externalities in the provision of water and sanitation services.

In May 1993 the federal government awarded a 30-year concession contract to the consortium. Although the contract did not specify required investment levels, it set gradual performance targets for such parameters as water and sanitation coverage (percentage of population served), percentage of wastewater to receive primary and secondary treatment, percentage of water and sanitation network to be renovated, and maximum percentage of unaccounted-for water. It also spelled out general water service levels and required that all investments be bid out. The targets set for the first 15 years of the concession imply the connection of about 1 million inhabitants every 5 years to the water supply and sewerage systems. The investment required to comply with these performance targets is an estimated US$100 million a year.

What is not clear in the concession contract are the consequences of failing to comply with the performance targets. This lack of clarity will weaken compliance unless the consortium finds the targets profitable. The operator was required to put up a US$150 million performance bond as security for the first five-year period. Aside from default, however, the level of underperformance that would trigger loss of the bond is unclear. For example, in

1996 the government regulator, Ente Tripartita de Servicios Sanitarios (ETOSS), began pressuring Aguas Argentinas to return revenues linked to contractually allowed price increases, because it claimed that the operator had not complied with contractually agreed-upon investment targets. Not surprisingly, the operator contested the claim. A compromise was reached, and the fee charged to the users for future investments was dropped.

Under the concession, Aguas Argentinas assumed full responsibility for the entire water supply and sanitation system, including commercial and technical operation and maintenance of all components. It must also finance and execute the investments needed to achieve service targets as specified in the contract. In addition, Aguas Argentinas assumed all financial risk and can disconnect users who do not pay their bills. As is usually the case with franchise bidding, additional regulation was kept to a minimum. Under contract provisions, rates are based on a cost-plus system, and water rates will be reassessed every five years based on the next five-year investment plan and updated spending estimates. An inflation index formula specified in the contract enables the regulatory institution, ETOSS, to monitor cost increases. The contract stipulates that rates can be revised only if cost increases due to inflation exceed 7 percent.

In July 1994, a little more than a year after the concession was granted, the tariff was renegotiated, and ETOSS granted an increase of 13.5 percent. Apparently this increase was granted partly because the government wanted to expedite investments (particularly in sanitation) and to replace nitrate-contaminated wells within the next few years and partly because labor costs were increasing faster than under the inflation formula included in the contract. This example illustrates one of the shortcomings of franchise bidding. When incentives for renegotiation are not properly addressed, the original bidding—the strong point of franchise bidding regulation—can be rendered almost meaningless. In other words, it becomes a matter not of potential efficiency but rather one of competence and expected renegotiation.

A No-Risk Airport Concession in Colombia

This example illustrates a concession that has not had any problems—except for a potentially higher tax burden—as a result of generous and riskless contract terms. In late 1993 the government of Colombia corporatized its Civil Aviation Authority, separating airport operations from air navigation activities. At the same time, it began developing a second runway at El Dorado International Airport in Bogota using a BOT scheme for construction and maintenance (as well as for maintenance of the existing runway).

The concessionaire's investment and operating costs, financing expenses, and profits are to be covered by landing fee revenues, which the Civil Aviation Authority will provide during the 20-year concession. Once bidders had fulfilled technical requirements, they were evaluated based on the net present value of the minimum landing fee revenue they would require throughout the concession period. In 1995 the government awarded the BOT concession, stipulating investments of US$97 million, to the consortium of Ogden, Dragados, and Conconcreto.

In a rare case of a government accepting commercial risk, the government has guaranteed a minimum level of revenue (floor pricing). If the landing fee structure, traffic volume, or both cannot support the required revenue stream, the government will compensate the concessionaire from a trust fund equivalent to 30 percent of annual landing fee revenue. This concession appears to be almost risk-free, and although it has been effective in the sense that no problems have arisen, the concern is whether the implicit higher taxpayer or user costs are necessary and appropriate.

Guaranteed Profits for Road Concessions in the Dominican Republic

The Dominican Republic has long granted risk-free road and railway concessions through direct adjudication rather than through competitive processes. Under these contracts, if ventures are not profitable or their costs exceed original estimates, Dominican taxpayers must cover the losses, because the contracts guarantee the earnings of the concessionaires.

An example is the Samana highway, which is the country's only toll road construction concession as of 2002. The contract for the highway stipulates that 6,050 vehicles will use it in its first year of the concession (2001) and that traffic will increase by 5 percent a year thereafter. If traffic does not reach those levels, the government will have to pay the winning bidder the shortfall in toll revenue. The government is also responsible for covering any deficits created by inflation, devaluation of the peso, and other cost-increasing components.

Historically, roads in the Dominican Republic have cost much more than their original budgets. Concession contracts allow operators to raise tolls as they see fit—but if users resist high tolls and decide to use other roads, the government is ultimately responsible for covering shortfalls in toll revenue. Yet in recent years, the Dominican Republic has been a leader among Latin American and Caribbean countries in terms of macroeconomic performance; annual growth rates have exceeded 5 percent. So, with relatively low risks, the question is whether direct adjudication and risk-free concession terms are appropriate. Although the generous terms of the Samana highway concessions create no reason to renegotiate the contract, this approach is a questionable way of avoiding renegotiation, and it adversely affects Dominican taxpayers.

Murky Selection Criteria in Choosing a Telecommunications Provider in Guatemala

Multiple contract award criteria can create problems, because they make ratings of bids highly subjective and arbitrary. For example, in 1995 Guatemala relied on a state-owned monopoly, the Guatemala Telephone Company (GUATEL), to provide fixed-line telephone services. The company's performance was dismal, with a national penetration rate (measured in terms of telephone lines per inhabitant) of less than 2 percent—ranging from 7 percent in Guatemala City to less than 0.5 percent in rural areas. As a result Guatemala had the second lowest penetration rate in Central America (after Honduras). Even though Guatemala is home to 10 million people, it had just 2,100 public telephones. Moreover, for households to get telephones took 2 to 20 years.

GUATEL was also extremely inefficient and has 230 employees per 10,000 phone lines. By contrast, telephone service providers in Japan and Spain have two to three employees per 10,000 lines. Nevertheless, GUATEL was highly profitable and had returns on equity reaching 80 percent in 1992. The company managed to achieve high profits despite low service quality, because it was a monopoly that charged extremely high prices, especially for international calls. A 10-minute call to the United States cost US$25, to South America US$45, and to Europe US$62. Because local services were not profitable, GUATEL had no incentive to develop its local network except in high-income areas.

GUATEL's monopoly was not seriously challenged by other technologies or providers. In mid-1994 COMCEL, a private operator, held the country's only license to provide cellular services—but after six years of operation, it had just 12,000 customers. Thus the government decided to promote competition by licensing a second cellular provider. But GUATEL, as the regulatory entity, was responsible for adjudicating the new license, and not until mid-1995 did it provide guidelines for the new bidding.

The bidding was to be adjudicated by the Receiving, Qualifying, and Adjudicating Commission (Comisión Receptora, Calificadora y Adjudicadora), which was composed of GUATEL employees. Eleven firms expressed interest in bidding, and seven offered bids. In August 1995 the commission granted the license to Mastec. But the award was based on nothing but murky promises about new technologies, coverage and service levels, and payment arrangements (see box 4.2).

Box 4.2 *Receiving, Qualifying, and Adjudicating Commission Report, August 18, 1995*

Technical Justifications

1. The design of the interconnection network and base stations is well defined, according to the bases required by GUATEL.
2. The design of the interconnection network includes circuits to all base stations.
3. The telecommunications infrastructure to achieve interconnection with the fixed-link network is independent of GUATEL's network, achieving the necessary network autonomy.
4. The bidder's proposed network is of medium capacity, ensuring the transportation of the traffic generated by cellular users.
5. The bidders' proposal considers power coverage levels between –75 dBm and –105 dBm, making the service useful for urban and rural areas.
6. The bidders' proposal offers a dual advanced mobile phone service–time division multiple access technology system, allowing digital or analog access and providing customers with more and better services.
7. The design includes a detail of spectrum use.
8. The design satisfies the requested level of service, thus ensuring quality of service.
9. For interconnection, the bidders' proposal considers redundant circuits for signaling and synchronization.
10. The bidders' proposal plans to cover the highway from the capital, Guatemala City, to Puerto Barrios in the inauguration.
11. The bidders' proposal plans good coverage (including more localities than required) for the inauguration.
12. The bidders' proposal accepts various providers of terminal equipment and detail percentage use of some of the more important ones.
13. The bidders plan higher than required reliability, complementing the quality of service.
14. The bidders' proposal offers a shorter execution plan than required in the bases.
15. The bidders' proposal considers a relatively high average coverage per year (41,005).

Economic and Financial Considerations

Mastec's marketing plan includes publicity campaigns using mass communications (radio and newspapers). . . . equipment distribution will be undertaken by third parties. . . . such as Radio Shack. . . . It also proposes that GUATEL be a distributor, providing it with commissions.

(Box continues on the following page.)

Box 4.2 *(continued)*

Apart from that, Mastec. . . . provides the best economic and financial conditions, being the first one of highest weight because they are linked to the economic and social activity of the state, given that the tariffs that the company offers to charge are the most favorable for the user. . . . Furthermore, it must be mentioned that Mastec is the one that offers the best payment to GUATEL. . . . It should be mentioned that this was not the point that most influenced the evaluation, but the previously mentioned [the tariffs] did. In terms of the financial analysis, . . . it is the one that presents the best indicators, thus we conclude, taking into consideration the points for the areas of technical and economic and financial feasibility that Mastec de Guatemala Sociedad Anónima must be the licensee.

Source: Crónica, September 29, 1995, p. 19. Translated and edited by the author.

Soon after, GUATEL's board of directors invalidated the commission's determination, claiming (among other things) that Mastec was not legally incorporated and citing uncertainty about its ability to deliver the promised services. (See *Crónica,* "Licitacion de Bandas," June 25, 1995, p. 37, "Otra Mano Peluda", September 29, 1995, p. 19, and "Hubo Mano de Mano," September 29, 1995, p. 26, for a description of the licensing process and subsequent problems.) The board then offered a different evaluation of each bidder, qualifying two previously disqualified bidders and giving Guacel—a company that made a very poor showing in the first round of bidding—the highest ranking in the second round, beating out the second-ranked bidder in the first round by less than one point.

Table 4.2 shows the points that each company received in the first and second rounds of the bidding. The board of GUATEL invalidated the commission's determination, however, claiming, among other things, that the winning company was not legally incorporated. Many other reasons for the decision of GUATEL's board were cited, including uncertainty about the company's ability to deliver the promised service. The board then instructed the commission to reconsider its determination. The board did so and offered a different evaluation of each of the bidders. It now qualified two of the previously disqualified bidders and gave Guacel, a company that had a very poor showing in the first round, the highest value, exceeding the previous number two by less than one point.

Table 4.2 *Points Granted to Each Bidder*

Bidder	First round	Second round
Mastec	88.75	Disqualified
Guacel	69.01	85.46
Londrina	84.90	84.49
Companias Electricas	51.42	56.10
Unicom	Disqualified	33.37
Semelec	Disqualified	32.20
BSC	Disqualified	Disqualified

Source: Crónica, September 29, 1995, p. 19.

As a result the bidding process produced three winners: the top-ranked bidder in the first round, the second-ranked bidder in the first round, and the top-ranked bidder in the second round. Each of the three publicly claimed that they were the winner. The two losers from the first round filed lawsuits, and after substantial discussion in the press and elsewhere, GUATEL canceled the licensing procedure altogether. After the cancellation, the winner in the second round also filed a lawsuit, requesting that it be given what it legally deserved.

As a result no license was granted until all three legal challenges made their way through the courts. In the meantime, GUATEL did not collect its licensing fees, and the commencement of competition with COMCEL and GUATEL was delayed. Indeed, licenses for personal communications services ended up being granted before the second cellular license.

The commission's reasons for changing the values of the bids were not clear. Although good reasons for such changes may exist, the subsequent evolution of the licensing process shows the problems associated with granting licenses not based on objective criteria.

The discretion granted to GUATEL would in most circumstances raise questions about undue influence. These problems may be even more extreme in countries with little or no experience in administrative procedures and administrative law. Thus in those countries, spectrum allocations must not be based on administrative-intensive procedures, but rather on auctions requiring little or no administrative capability.

Auctioning to the highest bidder is one such system. In Guatemala Mastec was also the company that claimed to have submitted the highest bid. According to GUATEL, Mastec's offer was for US$57.3 million—US$22 million in cash and the rest in kind, including a closed digital cellular network for exclusive government use (valued by Mastec at US$29.5 million), a national radio communication network, and 2,000 handsets for exclusive police use (the latter two valued by Mastec at US$5.8 million). This in-kind offer was another reason for disqualifying Mastec, because GUATEL's terms of reference had not called for any in-kind payments. Furthermore, Mastec's offer was not directed to GUATEL.

Similar problems occurred in the concession of an airport in Costa Rica, where multiple award criteria again created problems. Here the second-ranked bidder questioned the bid rankings, leading to a long delay while the dispute made its way through the courts.

Sharp Tariff Increases and Water and Sanitation Concession Termination in Bolivia

Some private schemes have encountered difficulties because of poor design—failing to account for user responses to sharp tariff increases and not phasing in and managing the reform. The water concession in Cochabamba, Bolivia, operated from October 1999 to April 2000, when it was terminated by the government following violent protests. Steep initial tariff increases were introduced at the outset to pay for an expensive bulk water scheme chosen by the government over a lower cost option. These high tariffs were unanticipated by consumers, and the chosen scheme, the planned tariff increases, and the financial terms of the concession seemed to have lacked transparency.

Government Failure to Honor Contract Clauses

Despite the technical and economic improvements often provided by concessionaires, many have had trouble ensuring that governments honor the terms of concession contracts. Changes in the rules of the game induce uncertainty and create risk, discouraging potential bidders and sometimes leading winning bidders to abandon concessions.

Refusals to Adjust Water Tariffs in Brazil

The archetypal case is Limeira, Brazil, where the concessionaire (Aguas de Limeira) was not permitted to adjust tariffs for inflation from the outset of the concession—even though this adjustment should have been automatic under the terms of the contract (Hughes 1999). Even worse for the general stability of concession contracts throughout Brazil, the concessionaire's applications to adjust tariffs were refused by local, state, and federal courts. The courts' unwillingness to enforce unambiguous contract terms provides an open invitation to behind-the-scenes negotiations that disregard the letter and intent of contracts and invariably result in deals that work against the interests of customers.

The mayor of Limeira argued that the concession was based on an unfair contract approved by a previous administration that did not take into account the municipality's long-run interests. Some of the criticisms were reasonable—such as those about the absence of annual payments for use rights and about the previous administration's failure to deal with workers not transferred to the concessionaire. But water and sanitation is a capital-intensive business, and part of the reason for seeking private participation is to mobilize investment. Such investment will not be forthcoming if every new municipal administration insists on renegotiating long-term contracts. Investors and lenders would be irresponsible if they invested in immobile assets without adequate contractual security to protect them from unilateral (and probably unfavorable) changes in operating conditions and contract terms. Reflecting such uncertainty, Aguas de Limeira suspended most new investments after the first two years of its contract, continuing only with those that produced a rapid return.

Some analysts argue that Brazilian law provides strong protection for concessionaires through the financial-economic equilibrium of the contract. In principle this assessment may be true, but in reality the interpretation of this concept is so open to dispute that much more time may be required to resolve legal issues than many concessionaires can manage. Aguas de Limeira is fortunate in having taken over a system with high levels of water and sewer coverage in a region with relatively high incomes. As a result nonpayment was low, and the utility was operating with positive cash flow even after three years without a tariff adjustment—though tariffs would be more than 50 percent higher if the inflation adjustment had been approved. Most concessionaires are in a much worse position. Even Aguas de Limeira has found itself in a difficult position as a result of the unresolved conflict. The consequences of the delays in settling legal disputes between concessionaires and governments are classic examples of the aphorism that justice delayed is justice denied.

Even though the case of Limeira is exceptional in terms of the length and severity of the dispute between the two parties, other examples of similar difficulties in the implementation of contract terms abound. In most the concessionaire has had to go to court to seek redress for actions by municipal authorities that violate the terms of the contract.

Problems with Water and Sanitation Concessions in Mexico

During the 1990s a number of Mexican states and municipalities seeking improvements and investments in water and sanitation services engaged private sector participation. Most was in the form of BOT contracts for water treatment plants. Many of those concessions went wrong; some were renegotiated and some discontinued. Reasons varied, but common ones included municipalities being unable to pay the contracted fees for treated water or dishonoring the contract, firms seeking higher fees, and governments seeking lower fees.

Termination of a Water and Sanitation Contract in Tucuman, Argentina

In 1994 the province of Tucuman, Argentina, auctioned the provision of its water and sanitation services. (This section is adapted from Artana, Navajas and Urbizondo 1998.) Only one bidder, Compañía de Aguas del Aconquija (CAA)—a joint venture between one French and three Argentine companies—participated in the auction, and in July 1995 it began operations under a 30-year concession. After the government accepted CAA's technical proposal, the company agreed to reduce from 94 to 68 percent its requested increase in the average water and sanitation tariff.

In March 1996, however, the provincial government threatened to terminate CAA's contract. The firm responded by applying for protection of its investments under an Argentine-French treaty. Negotiations between CAA and the provincial government continued in the face of political pressure to lower tariffs and campaigns encouraging users not to pay water bills. Even though the contract allowed it to do so, CAA did not suspend services to households in arrears—probably as part of its negotiation strategy. As a result arrears on water bills increased from 38 percent at the start of the concession to 75 percent in December 1997.

In 1997 two unexpected events led to the cancellation of the concession:

- In October 1995 a new government took office in Tucuman, and in December 1995 the provincial congress passed a resolution limiting the increase in the average tariff to 35 percent until a new tariff was negotiated. In January 1996 the public agency that reviews the legal aspects of public decisions in Tucuman decided that the agreed-upon 68 percent increase in the average tariff included provincial and local sales taxes, but CAA felt that any such indirect taxes should be in addition to its tariff.

- In late January 1996 manganese was found in Tucuman's main water source. Although CAA had to comply with quality targets that stipulated a maximum level of manganese and the company was not responsible for the affected water source, public confidence in CAA was shaken when water changed to a dark brown color. (CAA argued that manganese levels were not a priority because, under the concession contract, they had to be measured only once a month.)

After these incidents both CAA and the government of Tucuman sought to terminate the concession. Under the contract CAA was forced to continue providing services for 18 more months, until the government found a new supplier. Finally, in 1999 CAA abandoned the concession and the government took over operations.

Throughout this episode, CAA's strategy was to negotiate with the government. But the government's threats to cancel the concession because of the deterioration in water quality—without following the steps prescribed in the contract—indicate its intention to politicize the conflict. So do its claims that the increase in the average tariff included indirect taxes, because the contract was clear that provincial and municipal taxes were not costs to the firm and were to be passed on to consumers. The contract also required the wining bidder to maintain on its payroll at least 90 percent of the employees of the regulatory agency overseeing water services. Given the traditional overstaffing of public enterprises, this requirement would require a higher average tariff.

In addition to political conflicts between entering and departing governments, other reasons for the disputes with the CAA contract included the lack of transparency in tariff negotiations and the higher tariffs needed to finance CAA's ambitious investment program (which increased the likelihood of customer noncompliance with bill payments).

This case illustrates the challenges of securing financing for important sunk investments and ensuring the sustainability of high tariffs in the face of significant changes in government and insufficient competition in the award process. Despite the use of several standard instruments—such as reserving a portion of the firm's equity for employees, having a relatively well-designed regulatory agency, and limiting regional cross-subsidies—the privatization failed. Among the pitfalls that contributed to this failure was the requirement that 90 percent of regulatory staff remain employed in the new company, implying a higher tariff. Moreover, CAA accepted the requirement that it negotiate bilaterally with the government from the beginning. Finally, the fact that the regulatory agency was local may have encouraged politicization of the conflict.

Regulatory Surprises in a Cellular Telephone Contract in Ukraine

In 1997 the Ukrainian government decided to award, by tender, two frequencies to launch cellular phone networks. The hotly disputed tenders were awarded to two consortiums, one led by Motorola and one by Deutsche TeleKom AG. Both pledged to invest more than US$500 million in the networks.

After announcing the winners, the government changed the rules of the tender by demanding a US$65 million annual frequency fee from each of the winners—not a trivial amount considering that in 1996 the total revenue of the country's largest mobile phone operator was less than US$50 million. Moreover, the government had assured the bidders that no such fee would be imposed. Then, without notice, the government awarded a third frequency to a domestic company, Kievstar, with no known sources of financing or operational experience in telecommunications. The government also put the frequency allocations on hold for five months, presumably to allow the domestic company to catch up. As a result Motorola pulled out of the investment.

A Shortened Port Concession in Peru

In 1999 Peru began concessioning its regional ports, starting with the relatively small port of Matarani. The contract stipulated a 30-year concession, and four firms prequalified. During the countdown period, the last month prior to the opening of the bids, however, the government decided to shorten the concession to 15 years. As a result three of the firms withdrew from the process—not so much because of the shortened period, but because of the indication that the contract terms could be subject to unilateral changes, increasing uncertainty and risk. The concession was then awarded to the remaining bidder, a local economic group, at about the base price.

Defective Regulation and Its Effects

Many of the design problems described above have been exacerbated by a lack of proper regulation. Aside from the obvious problems when explicit regulatory framework is lacking, the types of problems can be legal, institutional, administrative, and enforcement-related. Some concessions have been granted in the absence of sector laws and even regulatory agencies. And in many cases regulatory agencies' structure, jurisdiction, and administrative capacity have been deficient, and resources have been sorely lacking. Such shortcomings mean that no competent neutral party reviews the design and oversees the development of and compliance with concession contracts. Those shortcomings not only facilitate renegotiation and arbitrary or political decisions, but leave transparency and predictability to the regulatory process and wrest compliance with the agreed-upon terms in the contract from either of the two parties.

Profile of a Typical Municipal Concession: Common Problems of Process and Design

To illustrate how a concession design affects the success of the transaction and operations and to point out the faulty processes often used, box 4.3 describes how, unfortunately, a number of concessions have been granted and the likely consequences.

Macroeconomic Shocks

For most concession operators, investments and obligations are in foreign currency, and revenues are in local currency. Thus when a destination country is subjected to a major shock, such as a devaluation, a concessionaire suffers a major blow to its financial viability. Although ideally concession contracts should specify the responses to such shocks, they often do not. Such shocks provide a reasonable justification to renegotiate tariffs, however.

An example is when Argentina abandoned its Convertibility Law in December 2001, triggering a major devaluation. In just a few months the Argentine peso went from being equivalent (one to one) to the U.S. dollar to trading at more than three pesos to the dollar. The government recognized the problem facing concessionaires—but, fearing a public outcry if tariffs were to increase considerably, took its time addressing the issue. Indeed, by February 2003 the issue still had not been resolved. A similar but lesser impact was felt in Mexico as a result of its 1994 financial crisis, which affected a number of road and water concessions.

Some high-profile private infrastructure schemes show what happens when politicians refuse to raise tariffs despite economic and financial realities, or when private investors have been given extremely generous terms for a variety of sometimes questionable reasons. For example, many analysts hoped that independent power projects would promote reform in countries that adopted this approach. The expectation was that the higher tariffs under these projects would support reform and ultimately place power sectors on sustainable financial footing.

Box 4.3 *How Municipal Concessions Are Often Awarded*

Note: All the names and events described in this box are purely fictional, and no inferences should be drawn from any similarities between them and actual people, companies, or events.

The municipality of Pueblo Latino has a population of about 250,000 and has been governed for many years by successive mayors from the same party. Water and sanitation services in the municipality is provided by CORFAE, which operates as an autarchy controlled by the municipality. CORFAE has 450 employees and reports that 80 percent of the population of the municipality is connected to piped water supply and 30 percent to sewers, although none of the sewage collected is treated before it is discharged into the Rio Latino. The water system is, at best, unreliable in many neighborhoods and does not work at all for long periods during the dry season. Total water losses, both technical and commercial, exceed 50 percent of the volume of water treated, and CORFAE manages to collect only 40 percent of the sums invoiced for water and sanitation services. Tariffs for industrial customers are high, and the current mayor is disappointed at the reaction of potential investors concerning the cost and availability of water supplies.

One day the mayor is approached by a group of business acquaintances—many of them with connections in the construction and engineering business—who suggest that he should establish a private concession for water and sanitation services. They point out the political benefits of the improvements that could be made by a concessionaire with funds to invest in expanding coverage. Furthermore, they indicate that the mayor might expect to receive significant contributions to his re-election campaign if he goes ahead with the concession. After some discussion, the mayor is convinced of the merits of the proposal, but he expresses concern about the capacity of the municipal administration to manage the process and says that no money is available to hire consultants. No problem, replies the leader of the group, we and our associated companies would be happy to provide the necessary technical expertise without charge.

The bidding documents, concession contract, and other materials are prepared by consultants whose main experience lies in the design of civil works projects. Thus, the documents focus heavily on schedules of investments and technical criteria and include little detail on service standards and goals, rules for adjusting and revising tariffs, regulation, contract enforcement, and dispute resolution. The process of awarding the concession takes the form of a "competition" rather than an "auction," and the results of a technical evaluation of proposals are given a much greater weight than the financial proposal in determining the winner. Prequalification requirements, especially in terms of experience of providing water and sanitation services, are generally low, but they include some highly technical conditions on financial status that can be used to disqualify unwanted bidders. To minimize the up-front commitment of capital, the financial proposal is based on the lowest tariff with a predefined tariff structure.

The mayor submits a law to the municipal council authorizing the award of a private concession. Some opposition councilors protest that the privatization is a bad deal for the municipality, but they are either persuaded to withdraw their objections or are isolated. After some delay, caused by various lawsuits, the bidding process gets under way. Fifteen copies of the bidding documents are sold, but only four consortia submit prequalification documents. Of these, one is disqualified, and the remaining three submit their technical and financial proposals. One of the bidders is disqualified on the grounds that its technical proposal does not achieve the minimum value required for its financial proposal to be considered. The financial envelopes of the remaining two bidders are opened and the evaluation committee declares that a consortium representing the group who originally approached the mayor has been awarded the concession. The other bidder does not protest, because in reality, it is allied with the winning consortium and has made a deal to obtain a large construction contract in a neighboring municipality. After further delays prompted by challenges to the outcome of the bidding process, the concession contract is signed by the mayor and the winning consortium, which takes over the concession immediately.

The new concessionaire offers jobs to 60 of the original employees of CORFAE, but only 30 accept the new terms and conditions. An additional 100 employees of CORFAE turn out to be "shadow" or retired workers, so that the former company is left with 320 employees, costing the municipality about US$ 4.5 million per year. Because elections are due within a year, the mayor decides that these surplus employees should not be made redundant.

In the first six months of its concession, the concessionaire invests US$4 million to upgrade the capacity and operations of its water treatment plant and distribution system. By the end of this period, 90 percent of the population have access to reliable and good quality water 24 hours per day, and no shortages occur during the dry season for the first time in many years. Further investments extend the water distribution system to cover over 95 percent of the population, although the coverage level for sewers increases more slowly.

After making these initial improvements, the concessionaire initiates a publicity campaign that stresses the benefits of reliable and good quality water supplies. At the same time it starts to pursue more aggressively those who fail to pay their bills. After a warning notice has been issued, households are cut off if they fail to pay their bills within 35 days. Industrial plants who do not pay are more of a problem because they lobby the mayor, claiming that they will be forced to sack workers if they have to pay the water prices specified in the concession contract.

(Box continues on the following page.)

Box 4.3 *(continued)*

Three months before the election, the mayor realizes that the contract allows the concessionaire to increase tariffs by 20 percent for cumulative inflation since bids were submitted. He refuses to authorize the tariff increase. Privately, he promises the concessionaire that its tariffs will be revised after the election to allow for inflation and for the shortfall in revenue from industrial plants. Unfortunately, despite his efforts the mayor is defeated by one of the opposition councilors who objected to the award of the concession.

Six months into the term of the new mayor, the concessionaire approaches him requesting either an adjustment or a revision in tariffs together with various other contract changes. The mayor points out that the municipal budget is heavily burdened by the cost of paying former employees of CORFAE, and the concession contract does not require the concessionaire to pay an annual canon to the municipality. A lengthy period of official and private negotiations ensues.

Eventually, the concessionaire agrees to pay an annual canon of 4 percent of gross invoices to the municipality, which is charged as a supplement to customer bills. In addition, the mayor authorizes a revision of tariffs equivalent to an increase of 30 percent in the average tariff, about 5 percent more than is strictly necessary to compensate for inflation and the revenue shortfall. The local newspaper reports that the mayor has recently started to spend his weekends at a large new house in a nearby beauty spot on the coast. On the basis of a lawsuit filed by a councilor from a member of the former ruling party, however, a local judge issues an injunction preventing the concessionaire from implementing the tariff increase on the grounds that the contract does not authorize the payment of a canon in the form of a tax on water and sanitation bills. The concessionaire decides to suspend all further investments until the dispute is resolved.

Source: Hughes (1999).

But in East Asia large devaluations revealed that the cost of capital was much higher than was incorporated into tariffs. Moreover, in the midst of a broader economic crisis, it proved impossible to impose sudden and large tariff adjustments to redress this shortfall. In Indonesia before the crisis, the unit costs of independent power projects ranged from US$0.054 to US$0.085 per kilowatt-hour, compared with an average retail tariff of US$0.07 per kilowatt-hour. When the value of the rupiah collapsed, even following steep electricity price hikes in early 1998, retail tariffs were less than $0.03 per kilowatt-hour, making the situation much worse.

In other countries, such as India and Pakistan, momentum was insufficient for reform to raise prices to cost-covering levels or to improve collections. More broadly, many renegotiations and some cancellations of independent power projects have occurred, reflecting difficulties in implementing and sustaining reforms in pricing and collections. But problems with independent power projects have often also arisen from the perceived generous terms of those contracts, and in some cases charges of corruption have been made. New administrations have questioned the high costs of these contracts and demanded renegotiation, as in the Dominican Republic. In 2002, the Dominican Republic refused to honor such contracts on the grounds of excessive terms, such as a power purchase agreement that charged more than US$0.10 per kilowatt-hour—as well as an independent power project that required the government to pay US$3.2 million a month even if the company delivered no electricity.

5

Renegotiation in Theory and Practice

A theory of optimal contracting predicts that even if parties cannot commit not to renegotiate, a contract will never be renegotiated if it specifies all possible contingencies and contains a full description of the renegotiation process. Thus renegotiation can be seen as resulting from incomplete contracts.

Reasons for Incomplete Contracts

Incomplete contracts have many causes. The first is the inability or costliness of accounting for all possible contingencies in contracts. Agents are not able to describe all the possible contingencies that could affect the functioning of the contract. Moreover, some contract contingencies cannot be verified by third parties, such as a contingency based on the concessionaire's level of exerted effort. In such cases writing a clause that includes effort level is useless, because such a clause cannot be enforced. Other contingencies cannot even be foreseen. Finally, writing a contract contingent on all verifiable and foreseeable contingencies may be too costly. Thus parties have to decide which contingencies they want to include.

A second reason is that contracting parties are not completely rational. A rational agent would be able to identify all the possible options relevant for decisionmaking and establish a well-defined order among them. Even though a good theory of bounded rationality does not exist, and most models that deal with it have been criticized for being ad hoc, the truth is that in complex contexts, agents often make mistakes and need a learning period to approach an optimal solution. Of course, the learning period creates intermediate suboptimal results that must be remedied over time. Thus renegotiation can be seen as a way of correcting past mistakes.

Another aspect that must be taken into account is that governments have multiple (and sometimes incompatible) objectives, and new governments might have different objectives than previous ones. Thus a privatization program might have multiple and inconsistent objectives, and contracts must make tradeoffs among these divergent objectives. Renegotiation may simply reflect a change in government objectives, especially after a change in government. (This hypothesis is supported by the fact that many renegotiations have been initiated by governments, often new ones.)

Finally, the degree of government commitment helps determine the nature of the contract and influences the probability of renegotiation. A large portion of concessionaires have been selected through competitive auctions, to choose the most efficient firm to run the concession. As noted, however, bidders have often anticipated the possibility of renegotiation and based their bids not only on their costs, but also on the costs of securing the concession. At the auction stage, bidders take into account their potential market power once they enter an industry as well as their bargaining power at the renegotiation stage. Underbidding increases the probability of winning an auction, and the possibility of renegotiation reduces the losses associated with it. In the period between the award of a concession and renegotiation, the winning firm increases its bargaining power and so is able to obtain a better deal. Thus renegotiation may occur because a government is not able to refuse it.

Incomplete Contracts, Concession Successes and Failures, and the Theory of Renegotiation

How do different factors contribute to the success or failure of a concession, influencing the incidence of renegotiation? Here a concession is considered a failure if renegotiation occurs during the concession's contracted period of operation. The theoretical foundations of renegotiation have been developed in Aghion, Dewatripont, and Rey (1994); Bajari and Tadelli (2000); Banerjee and Duflo (2002); Battigalli and Maggi (2000); Dewatripont (1988); Engel, Fischer, and Galetovic (1996, 1997a,b, 2000, 2003); Green and Laffont (1992); Guasch, Kartacheva, and Quesada (2000); Guasch, Laffont, and Straub (2003); Hart and Moore (1988); Jeon and Laffont (1999); Laffont and Tirole (1993); Manelli and Vincent (1995); McAfee and McMillan (1986); Segal and Whinston (2002); Tirole (1986, 1999). Most of those models focus on how ex ante incentives affect ex post bargaining and renegotiation and provide testable hypotheses that are accommodated as much as the data permit in the empirical estimates provided in this and the following chapters.

Contract incompleteness and renegotiation have been widely studied by economists in recent years. Most economists agree that most concession contracts are incomplete and that renegotiation is one way to redress inefficiencies caused by incompleteness. Yet no clear definition of "incomplete contracting" exists, and in most cases an incomplete contract is defined as one that imposes one or more ad hoc restrictions on the set of feasible contracts in a given model (Tirole 1999).

Transaction costs are most often argued to be the main reason for contract incompleteness. Three basic issues are involved here. First, contracting parties cannot define ex ante the contingencies that may occur after the signing of a contract. Thus the contracting parties may face unforeseen contingencies. Second, even if one could foresee all contingencies, they might be so numerous that describing them in a contract would be too costly, and the cost of writing contracts may lead to incompleteness. Finally, courts must perfectly understand the terms of a contract and be able to verify all actions under all contingencies to enforce it. If they do not satisfy some of these criteria, enforcing a contract will generate a cost.

The major paper in the literature is Hart and Moore (1988), who focus on the cost of writing a contingency clause in a sufficiently clear and unambiguous way that it can be enforced. When a state of nature—one of the contingent events—is realized, the parties always have a possibility to revise or renegotiate the initial contract, and the bargaining process is exogenous in the authors' model. When parties are risk-neutral and undertake relationship-specific investment, studies have shown that they will underinvest even if their actions are verifiable. In contrast to this result, Chung (1992, 1995) shows that if parties are risk-neutral, an efficient outcome can be induced if a contract specifies a quantity, a payment, and an ex post revision through a take-it-or-leave-it offer.

The main difference between these two papers lies in the fact that Hart and Moore assume that trade is voluntary and that the best a contact can do is specify "trade" and "no trade" prices, whereas Chung assumes that courts can enforce the initial allocation if requested to do so by one party, which puts a strict restriction on the revision stage. Aghion, Dewatripont, and Rey (1994) show that the underinvestment problem can be solved if renegotiation design is possible—that is, if it is possible to allocate all the bargaining power in the renegotiation game to one of the contracting parties and to specify a default point if the renegotiation breaks down. In this case the party with all the bargaining power in the renegotiation becomes a residual claimant on total surplus and has incentives for efficient investments. Incentives for the other party are provided through the effect of its investments on the default point. So, if a third party is able to exercise control over the bargaining process, which is the case in this study and Chung's, efficiency can be achieved.

The bounded rationality of players, which is rarely explicitly modeled, and imperfections of the judicial system are often suggested as reasons for contract incompleteness and renegotiation. But they are often assumed in a rather ad hoc way. Modeling more precisely the imperfections of the judicial system is certainly the most promising path in our state of knowledge. One simple way is to observe that many contracts call for ex post penalties and to stress the imperfect enforcement of those penalties. Bondt (2001) constructs a moral hazard model with ex post penalties that may not be enforced because of side contracting between judges and the contractual party to be punished. Anderlini, Felli, and Postlewaite (2000) instead consider incomplete contracts in which judges seeking to maximize social welfare may be willing to void some clauses, possibly leading to renegotiation. Laffont (2000) and Laffont and Meleu (2001) offer procurement and regulation models involving adverse selection, in which imperfect enforcement of penalties can be affected by expenditures on enforcement very much in the black box tradition of the Chicago school.

Green and Laffont (1992) consider a model with risk-neutrality and quasi-linear utility functions. Because renegotiation is always costly, an optimal contract entails an efficient outcome to be achieved without effective renegotiation. General utility functions or parties' risk aversion may impede efficient outcomes, however.

Closer to the context in this book, Jeon and Laffont (1999) and Bajari and Tadelli (2000) develop models showing the impact of risk allocation on renegotiation, with high-powered incentive schemes (such as price-cap regulation) leading to a higher incidence of renegotiation than low-powered incentive schemes (such as rate-of-return regulation). Those authors also show that strategic renegotiation is more likely with bank financing than with government financing or guarantees.

An additional explanation for renegotiation on the government's part, suggested by Engel, Fischer, and Galetovic (2003), is based on the political economy of budget allocations. The argument is based on the government bias toward anticipating spending so as to increase its chances of being reelected, and the mechanism to secure increased anticipated investments is through renegotiation of the contract. The government can use renegotiation of the concession contract to compel the concessionaire to finance and provide new public works and in exchange be compensated via higher tariffs or tolls, by being granted additional guarantees, or via extensions of the concession period. The granting of this compensation is done through an off the budget approval process and does not need to be approved by parliament or negotiated with the opposition. Indeed, there appears to be some empirical validation for this additional explanation for renegotiation, as seen in table 1.17. That table, which shows the common outcomes of renegotiation, indicates that in 18 percent of renegotiated concession contracts there are accelerations of or new investment obligations. It also indicates that in 38 percent of the cases the concession period is extended.

Guasch, Kartacheva, and Quesada (2000) show that expectations of renegotiation at the bidding stage and affiliation—a measure that indicates an operator's ability to renegotiate—may lead to firms with high affiliation and high costs winning auctions through low-ball bidding strategies. In that model each bidder has two main characteristics. The first is standard in the literature on adverse selection: a cost parameter, which is private information held by a bidder. If concession awards were based only on firms' marginal costs, auctions would lead to the most efficient firm becoming the operator of a concession. But bidders may also have different renegotiation skills because of an affiliation with the regulator or government (or both) or because of the indispensable nature of the concession, as with water and sanitation services. As a result a government may be locked into a relationship with an operator, and competition has little effect on the renegotiation process once a concession has been awarded. Renegotiation is then a bilateral negotiation between the operator and the government. So, the winning bidder's renegotiation skills and bargaining power already play an important role at the bidding stage.

The analysis shows that a winning bidder's anticipated high bargaining power after entering an industry may lead to strategic underbidding at the auction stage. As a result an inefficient firm with close affiliation to the regulator or government may become the operator of a concession. This result helps explain why many concessions in Latin America have been renegotiated just after the concession award. Similar outcomes are obtained if different bidders have different chances for a favorable renegotiation shortly after the award of a concession.

In trying to elicit the impact of award criteria on the likelihood of renegotiation, Guasch, Kartacheva, and Quesada (2000) also show that renegotiation is less likely if award criteria are highly dependent on information about bidding firms at the time of the auction and flexible in terms of tariff policy. That finding provides motivation for testing for the impact on renegotiation of the two most common criteria for awarding concessions: minimum tariffs and transfer fees. The results of such tests are quite strong and motivated the work of Engel, Fischer, and Galetovic (1996, 1997a,b, 2001). The authors' concern about renegotiation led them to develop a criterion that is renegotiation-proof: the least present value of revenue (LPVR), an extremely attractive mechanism that awards concessions to bidders that submit contracts with the LPVR.

Under that approach a concession has a flexible end point that comes when that revenue is secured. Any issue that leads to a shortfall in revenues is automatically handled by extending the length of the concession. The main drawbacks of this approach are that it is mostly applicable to concessions in which service quality does not affect demand, as with roads, bridges, and dams, and that it might affect the financing of the project because the duration of the concession is uncertain. Estache and Quesada (2001) develop a model to analyze the distributive impact of renegotiation and the equity and efficiency tradeoffs.

Guasch, Laffont, and Straub (2003) develop a theoretical framework that analyzes the impact of institutional constraints on the incidence of renegotiation. The focus is on state capture, corruption, macroeconomic shocks, and the quality of enforcement and the rule of law. Among the findings are the following:

- The higher the state capture is, the higher the probability of renegotiation is.
- The higher the costs of enforcing the contract are or the lower the quality of enforcement is, the higher the probability of renegotiation is.
- The higher the committed investments are, the higher the probability of renegotiation is, whereas private financing has an ambiguous effect.
- Because arbitration rules help settle disputes, making renegotiation less costly, the existence of formal arbitration rules increases the probability of renegotiation.
- The existence of a regulatory body at the time of a concession award decreases the probability of renegotiation.
- Minimum income guarantees decrease the probability of renegotiation, but they also decrease incentives for effort.

The theory of institutions also provides insights on the determinants of performance and possible renegotiation (see Guasch and Spiller 2001; Knack and Keefer 1995; Pritchett 2000; Smith 1997a,b,c). The focus here is on the impact of the structure of the regulatory framework and the quality of oversight and enforcement. The issues involved include the legal grounding of the regulatory framework, the autonomy of the regulatory agency (location, funding, operations), regulator attributes (including security of employment), appeals mechanisms, the discretion granted to the regulatory agency (in itself and in interpreting legal documents), and the overall openness and transparency of the regulatory process. When properly in place, all these elements limit the probability of capture and renegotiation and can provide certainty and predictability to all agents involved, particularly existing and potential investors.

To summarize, the economic literature suggests that incomplete contracts can lead to inefficiencies that are exacerbated by weak enforcement and in some cases can also lead to ex post inefficiencies that cannot be resolved even through renegotiation. The literature also shows that if government is politically constrained, it may tolerate imprecise information about the demand for a new market activity and delay corrections until the renegotiation stage. Aside from a number of unforeseen contingencies that have played important roles in the initiation of renegotiations, at the auction stage many firms have expected to engage in renegotiations and understood their ability to influence the outcomes, resulting in unrealistic bids that had to be revised just after the concessionaire started operation.

Renegotiation Issues in Latin America and the Caribbean

All these issues seem to have influenced concessions and privatizations in Latin America and the Caribbean. Moreover, governments overseeing concessions and privatizations have often faced political constraints. A common constraint was the goal of processing an ambitious concession or privatization program in the short span of a presidential term (usually about five years), because in many Latin American countries, immediate reelection was not possible. As a result enormous attention has often been devoted to the speed of the process, ignoring needed improvements in contract designs and necessary information about markets and firms, increasing the likelihood of incomplete contracts and facilitating renegotiation. Incomplete contracts may also have increased some operators' expectations of renegotiation and affected their bids.

For similar reasons the development of regulations has often lagged behind the concession program, increasing uncertainty, weakening enforcement, and facilitating renegotiation. Thus the theories discussed above provide a set of hypotheses that help explain renegotiation in Latin America and the Caribbean. This study uses those hypotheses to specify econometric models that are then tested using collected empirical evidence. The most salient of the hypotheses are the following:

- Higher quality enforcement of contract terms (as indicated by the existence and structure of a regulatory agency) reduces the incidence of renegotiation.
- Extensive corruption in a country increases the incidence of renegotiation.
- More extensive investment obligations in a contract (that is, regulation by means as opposed to regulation by objectives) increase the incidence of renegotiation.
- A larger share of risks allocated to operators increases the incidence of renegotiation.
- Closer affiliation between winning bidders and the government increases the incidence of renegotiation.
- Macroeconomic shocks increase the incidence of renegotiation.
- Minimum income guarantees decrease the incidence of renegotiation.
- Softer award criteria, in terms of commitment and financial costs at the transfer time (the lock-in effect), increase the incidence of renegotiation.
- Weak legal grounding for regulation increases the incidence of renegotiation.
- As the number of concessions granted in a country increases, the incidence of renegotiation decreases.
- A more competitive award process (as opposed to bilateral negotiation)—and its corollary, a large number of bidders—increases the incidence of renegotiation.
- Awarding concessions shortly before or shortly after elections increases the incidence of renegotiation.

6

Confirming Anecdote and Theory: Empirical Analysis of the Determinants of Renegotiation

To impute the determinants of renegotiation and to test the hypotheses provided by theory and empirical observations, data were collected on about 1,000 concession contracts awarded in Latin America and the Caribbean between the mid-1980s and 2000. That region was chosen because it has been the pioneer in awarding concessions; thus by 2000 many of its concessions had established track records.

The contracts in the sample include 17 countries in the region, and the concessions are fairly evenly distributed across the four main infrastructure sectors: telecommunications, energy, transportation, and water and sanitation. The dataset contains detailed information on the characteristics of these concessions, including general project details (sector, activity, year of award), award criteria, contract size and duration, information on the institutional context and degree of regulator freedom, type of regulatory framework (price cap, rate of return, or no regulation), and other details such as arbitration clauses and nationality of operators. (For complementary summary statistics from the dataset, see appendix 1.) Table 6.1 presents the number of concessions in the dataset by country and sector.

The timing of the concessions shows certain lumpiness in the concession program, such as in Argentina, Bolivia, Brazil, Peru, and Mexico, particularly, where most of the concessions were granted by a new reform-oriented administration that had a five-year mandate and wanted to complete the program within its tenure.

Table 6.1 *Number of Infrastructure Concessions in Latin America and the Caribbean by Country and Sector, Mid-1980s to 2000*

Country	Telecom- munica- tions	Energy	Transpor- tation	Water and sanitation	Total	Share of total (percent)
Argentina	17	31	40	14	102	10.8
Bolivia	0	17	5	2	24	2.5
Brazil	87	7	50	50	194	20.6
Chile	12	81	27	3	123	13.1
Colombia	0	0	44	7	51	5.4
Costa Rica	0	31	1	0	32	3.4
Dominican Republic	1	10	3	0	14	1.4
Ecuador	0	2	0	0	2	0.2
Guatemala	1	0	2	0	3	0.3
Honduras	1	8	0	1	10	1.0
Jamaica	2	0	0	0	2	0.2
Mexico	63	51	91	58	263	27.9
Panama	0	0	5	0	5	0.5
Peru	85	17	5	0	107	11.3
Trinidad and Tobago	1	1	0	1	3	0.3
Uruguay	0	0	2	1	3	0.3
Republica Bolivariana de Venezúela	3	0	1	0	4	0.4
Total	273	256	276	137	942	100.0
Share of total (percent)	28.9	27.1	29.2	14.5	100.0	

Source: Author's calculations.

Basic Findings

Here renegotiation is considered to have occurred if a concession contract underwent a significant change or amendment not envisioned or driven by stated contingencies. Examples include substantial changes in tariffs, investment plans and levels, exclusivity rights, guarantees, lump-sum payments or annual fees, coverage targets, service standards, and concession periods. Standard, scheduled tariff adjustments and periodic tariff reviews do not count as renegotiation.

Incidence of Renegotiation

Renegotiation was extremely common among the concessions in the sample, occurring in 30 percent of them (tables 6.2 and 6.3). Not including the concessions in the telecommunications sector, because practically all telecommunications projects were privatized rather than concessioned, raises the incidence of renegotiation to 41.5 percent. Renegotiation was especially common in transportation concessions, occurring in 55 percent, and even more so in water and sanitation concessions, occurring in 74 percent.

Renegotiation was far less common in telecommunications and energy, to some extent as a result of the more competitive nature of these sectors, which significantly reduces the leverage of concessionaires and bargaining powers for renegotiations. In most cases telecommunications and energy concessionaires are not the only service providers, giving governments more options for securing these services from other operators, existing or new, in the event of a threat by operators to abandon the concessions if renegotiation demands were not met.

Timing of Renegotiation

Most renegotiated concessions underwent renegotiation soon after their award, with an average of just 2.2 years between concession awards and renegotiations (table 6.4). Renegotiations came most quickly in water and sanitation concessions, occurring an average of 1.6 years after concession awards. Renegotiations of transportation concessions occurred after an average of 3.1 years, perhaps reflecting the sector's longer construction times. Moreover, the variance in the distribution of renegotiation periods was very small; 85 percent of renegotiations occurred within 4 years of

Table 6.2 *Incidence of Renegotiation Total and by Sector*

Incidence by sector	Total	Total (excluding telecommunications)	Electricity	Transportation	Water and sanitation
Percentage of renegotiated contracts	30	41.5	9.7	54.7	74.4

Source: Author's calculations.

Table 6.3 Number and Share of Renegotiated Concessions in Latin America and the Caribbean by Country and Sector, Mid-1980s to 2000

Country	Telecom-munications	Energy	Transport-ation	Water and sanitation	Total	Share of total (percent)	Total excluding telecom-munications	Share of total excluding telecom-munications (percent)
Argentina	0/17	0/31	34/40	11/14	45/102	44.1	45/85	52.9
Bolivia	0/0	2/17	0/5	1/2	3/24	12.5	3/24	12.5
Brazil	0/87	0/7	28/50	42/50	70/194	36.0	70/107	65.4
Chile	0/12	4/81	6/27	0/3	10/123	8.1	10/111	9.0
Colombia	0/0	0/0	28/44	0/7	28/51	54.9	28/51	54.9
Costa Rica	0/0	0/31	1/1	0/0	1/32	3.1	1/32	3.1
Dominican Republic	0/1	7/10	1/3	0/0	8/14	57.1	8/13	61.5
Ecuador	0/0	0/2	0/0	0/0	0/2	0.0	0/2	0.0
Guatemala	1/1	0/0	2/2	0/0	3/3	100.0	2/2	100.0
Honduras	0/1	6/8	0/0	0/1	6/10	60.0	6/9	66.6
Jamaica	0/2	0/0	0/0	0/0	0/2	0.0	0/0	0.0
Mexico	0/63	2/51	46/91	46/58	94/263	35.7	94/200	47.0
Panama	0/0	0/0	1/5	0/0	1/5	20.0	1/5	20.0
Peru	1/85	3/17	3/5	0/0	7/107	6.5	6/22	27.3
Trinidad and Tobago	0/1	1/1	0/0	1/1	2/3	66.7	2/2	100.0
Uruguay	0/0	0/0	0/2	1/1	1/3	33.3	1/3	33.3
Republica Bolivariana de Venezuela	1/3	0/0	1/1	0/0	2/4	50.0	1/1	100.0
Total	3/273	25/256	151/276	102/137	281/942	29.8	278/669	41.5
Renegotiation incidence (percent)	1.1	9.7	54.7	74.4	29.8			

Source: Author's calculations.

Table 6.4 *Average Time to Renegotiation since Award, Mid-1980s to 2000*
(years)

All renegotiated concessions	Transportation sector only	Water and sanitation sector only
2.2	3.12	1.60

Source: Author's calculations.

concession awards and 60 percent occurred within 3 years—for concessions that were supposed to run for 15–30 years (table 6.5).

Incidence of Renegotiation by Contract Award Process

Most of the concessions in the sample were awarded through competitive bidding rather than through direct adjudication and bilateral negotiation (table 6.6). Renegotiation was far less likely, however, in concessions awarded noncompetitively, occurring in just 8 percent of such contracts— compared with 46 percent for contracts awarded through competitive bidding (excluding the telecommunications concessions, table 6.7).

Type of Regulation

Most concessions, 56 percent, were regulated through a price-cap regime. About 20 percent of the concessions were regulated via a rate-of-return regime and about 24 percent had a hybrid regime (table 6.8).

Initiator of Renegotiation

In 61 percent of cases, concessionaries or operators requested renegotiation, and in 26 percent of the cases, the government initiated renegotiation

Table 6.5 *Small Variance of Time Distribution to Renegotiate, Mid-1980s to 2000*

Time interval to renegotiation	Percentage of contracts
Within first 4 years after concession award	85
Within first 3 years after concession award	60

Source: Author's calculations.

Table 6.6 *Number of Concessions by Award Process in Latin America and the Caribbean by Sector, Mid-1980s to 2000*

Award process	Telecom-munica-tions	Energy	Transpor-tation	Water and sanitation	Total	Share of total (percent)
Competitive bidding	245	95	231	125	696	78
Direct adjudication (bi-lateral negotiation)	15	143	37	4	199	22
Total	260	238	268	129	895	100

Note: A few concessions in the dataset were difficult to classify, and thus for this table they were left out.
Source: Author's calculations.

Table 6.7 *Percentage of Concessions Renegotiated According to Competitive or Noncompetitive Process, Excluding the Telecommunications Sector*

Incidence of renegotiation according to award process	Percentage of contracts
Renegotiation when awarded via competitive bidding	46
Renegotiation when awarded via bilateral negotiations	8

Source: Author's calculations.

Table 6.8 *Distribution of Concessions by Type of Regulation*
(percent)

Type of regulation	Frequency
Price cap	56
Rate of return	20
Hybrid[a]	24

a. Hybrid regimes are defined when, under a price-cap regulatory regime, a large number of costs components are allowed an automatic pass-through into tariff adjustments.
Source: Author's calculations.

(table 6.9). In the remaining cases, both the concessionaire and the government jointly sought renegotiation. When conditioned by the type of regulatory regime in place (table 6.10), one can see that operators were predominantly and almost exclusively the initiators of renegotiation (83 percent), whereas under a rate-of-return regime, the government led the

Table 6.9 *Who Initiated the Renegotiation?*
(percentage of total requests)

Sector	Both government and operator	Government	Operator
All sectors	13	26	61
Water and sanitation	10	24	66
Transportation	16	27	57

Source: Author's calculations.

Table 6.10 *Who Initiated the Renegotiation Conditioned on Regulatory Regime?*
(percentage of total requests)

Regulatory regime	Both government and operator	Government	Operator
Price cap	11	6	83
Rate of return	39	34	26
Hybrid regime	30	26	44

Source: Author's calculations.

request for renegotiation, but with a much lower incidence (34 percent). That discrepancy is partially explained by the increased risk to the operator of a price-cap regulatory regime.

Investment Obligations

Most concessions, 71 percent, had investment obligations with which the operator had to comply, and only about 13 percent had only performance or output indicators to be met. About 16 percent had both, investment obligations and output indicators (table 6.11).

Contract Features and the Incidence of Renegotiation

Renegotiation was far more likely (renegotiation occurred in 60 percent of cases) when concession contract awards were based on the lowest proposed tariff rather than on the highest transfer fee (11 percent); see table 6.12. Renegotiation was also much more likely when concession contracts contained investment requirements (70 percent) than when they included

Table 6.11 *Distribution of Concessions by Existence of Investment Obligations in Contract*
(percent)

Investment obligations versus performance indicators in concession contracts	Percentage of contracts
Investment obligations in contract	71
No investment obligations in contract but performance indicators	13
Hybrid	16

Source: Author's calculations.

performance indicators (18 percent). Moreover, the incidence of renegotiation was much higher under price-cap regulation (42 percent) than rate-of-return regulation (13 percent), and when a regulatory agency was not in place (61 percent) than when one was in place (17 percent). Finally,

Table 6.12 *Contract Features and the Incidence of Renegotiated Concessions in Latin America and the Caribbean, Mid-1980s to 2000*

Feature	Incidence of renegotiation (percent)
Award criteria	
Lowest tariff	60
Highest transfer fee	11
Regulation criteria	
Investment requirements (regulation by means)	70
Performance indicators (regulation by objectives)	18
Regulatory framework	
Price cap	42
Rate of return	13
Existence of regulatory body	
Regulatory body in existence	17
Regulatory body not in existence	61
Impact of legal framework	
Regulatory framework embedded in law	17
Regulatory framework embedded in decree	28
Regulatory framework embedded in contract	40

Source: Author's calculations.

renegotiation was more likely when the regulatory framework was embedded in the contract (40 percent) than when embedded in a decree (28 percent) or a law (17 percent). (The sectoral decomposition of the data shows similar patterns; see tables 6.13, 6.14 and appendix 1.)

Empirical Analysis of the Determinants of Renegotiation

To identify the determinants of renegotiation, the impact of various explanatory variables on the probability of renegotiation was estimated. The choice of the independent (explanatory) variables is guided by the theory of contracts and institutions described above. The hypotheses tested, driven by the theory, were the impact on the probability of renegotiation of macroeconomic shocks, enforcement quality, financial structure of the concession, extent of competition in the award process, extent of affiliation, award criteria, investment obligations, legal grounding of regulation, electoral cycles, risk allocations, and reputation and learning curve of the government. These factors and the variables and proxies used to evaluate their impact are described in appendix 2.

The estimation is a probit analysis. To ensure consistency, various models were sequentially tested to impute the significance and marginal impact of the key variables on the probability of renegotiation. The models, choices, and definitions of the explanatory variables; the methodology; and the econometric estimates of the probit analysis are presented in appendix 3. The estimation is complemented by a separate paper by Guasch, Laffont,

Table 6.13 *Transportation Sector Renegotiation Incidence and Average Time Until Renegotiation*

Renegotiated concessions	54.7 percent
Average time from award to renegotiation	3.1 years

Source: Author's calculations.

Table 6.14 *Water and Sanitation Sector, Incidence of Renegotiation, Average Time of Concession Until Renegotiation*

Incidence of renegotiation: 74.4%
Average time until renegotiation: 1.7 years

Source: Author's calculations.

and Straub (2003) that focuses on a narrower part of the dataset.[1] The dependent variable in all the models is the probability of renegotiation. The following summary of the main empirical results is broadly consistent with the predictions of the theory.

Significant Variables Influencing the Incidence of Renegotiation

The following variables tested with significant coefficients in the empirical analysis, that is, they are determinants of the probability of renegotiation:

- Macroeconomic shocks (including devaluations)
- Award criteria
- Investments required from concessionaire
- Extent of competition in concession award process
- Existence of regulatory body
- Autonomy of regulatory body
- Type of regulation
- Nationality of concessionaire (affiliation)
- Electoral cycles
- Source of project finance
- Number of prior concessions
- Length of concession
- Corruption.

These determinants of renegotiation can be grouped into the following categories:

- *Macroeconomic shocks.* Macroeconomic shocks considerably increase the likelihood of renegotiation, especially when the variable enters in lag form (see Guasch, Laffont, and Straub 2003).
- *Concession design.* The broad concept of concession design significantly affects the probability of renegotiation in at least three ways. The first is the choice of award criteria: criteria based on low tariffs,

---

1. Guasch, Laffont, and Straub (2003) focus on the Latin American and Caribbean countries where most concessions took place—Argentina, Brazil, Chile, Colombia, Mexico, and Peru—and on the two sectors that had the most concessions and were the most affected by renegotiation—transportation and water—and only on operator-led renegotiation, and deal extensively with the issue of endogeneity and on the impact of the party that led the renegotiation.

as opposed to transfer fees, increase the probability of renegotiation. The second is investment requirements, which also increase the probability of renegotiation. The third is the level of competition in the process: competitive bidding of concessions (as opposed to direct adjudication or bilateral negotiation) increases the probability of renegotiation. This last result should not be interpreted as suggesting that direct adjudication is preferable to competitive bidding, however—in fact, the opposite is true, as already explained.

- *Regulatory framework.* The regulatory framework significantly influences the incidence of renegotiation in two main ways. One is through the quality of enforcement, as measured by the existence and autonomy of a regulatory agency—both decrease the probability of renegotiation. The other is through the allocation of risks, as measured by the type of regulation. Price-cap regulation—in which the operator bears the risk—increases the probability of renegotiation relative to rate-of-return regulation.

- *Political and behavioral environment.* Three factors or proxies were used to measure expectations and likelihood of renegotiation, and all tested significant. The first was the affiliation variable, and the results indicate that having a local operator increases the probability of renegotiation. The second was the country's level of corruption: the more widespread the corruption, the higher the probability of renegotiation. The third was the impact of elections. With a lagged effect, an election year increased the probability of renegotiation—which helps explain the large number of government-led renegotiations, many politically motivated. Political cycles also have a significant effect: renegotiations are far more common in years immediately following national elections (even after controlling for economic cycles). This result can be related to the effect of state capture, meaning that as governments with close ties to firms assume power, they are more likely to tolerate renegotiations. A more detailed analysis of this aspect would need to consider the nature of political changes. In particular, asymmetries might appear depending on whether the previous government cared more or less for a concessionaire's rents than its successor (see Aubert and Laffont 2002). Finally, interactions between the nature of government and institutional characteristics, such as corruption, might also be relevant.

- *Other determinants.* Several other variables were also significant in the estimations. First, when project finance involves state funding, renegotiation is more likely. This relationship is a bit surprising, but a possible explanation is that having the government as a partner might make renegotiation easier. Second, a large number of prior concessions decreased the probability of renegotiation. This finding could imply a learning curve effect—that is, after a while, and perhaps in response to criticism, countries learn to address problems with concession contracts. Finally, longer concession periods lowered the probability of renegotiation. Other variables were tested, such as the impact of the number of bidders, but the results were inconclusive.

Marginal Effects on the Probability of Renegotiation

The probit estimates produced the marginal effects of these variables on the probability of renegotiation. The results from the various models tested were fairly consistent, and the variables that had the largest marginal effects and their ranges are described in table 6.15.

Interpretation of Empirical Results

The econometric estimates of the determinants of the renegotiation of concession contracts by and large corroborates the theory prescriptions described in the previous chapter. The interpretation of the results follows and is broken down into three key areas of impact: the role of regulation, the role of concession design, and the role of political influences.

Table 6.15 *Marginal Effects of Significant Variables on the Probability of Renegotiation*

Significant variables affecting the probability of renegotiation	Marginal effect on probability of renegotiation
Existence of regulatory body	20–40 percent
Award criteria	20–30 percent
Type of regulation	20–30 percent
Autonomy of regulatory body	10–30 percent
Investment obligations	10–20 percent
Nationality of concessionaire	10–20 percent
Extent of competition in award process	10–20 percent
Macroeconomic shocks (devaluations)	10–15 percent
Electoral cycles	3–5 percent
Award process	10–20 percent

Source: Author.

Role of Regulation

The interpretation and intuition behind the results are fairly clear. As expected, the existence and type of regulation are highly significant in explaining renegotiation incidence. Both are proxies for the quality of enforcement, and better enforcement—through the presence of a neutral professional institution that can evaluate an operator's status and claims—should dissuade or reject inappropriate claims for renegotiation. In addition, a stronger legal grounding for regulation (embedded in a law rather than in a decree or contract) lessens the probability of renegotiation and increases the political cost of government-led renegotiation.

In terms of the autonomy of the regulatory body, the findings provide little support for the notion that an independent body is crucial in limiting renegotiation. In the specifications tested, the sign of the corresponding variable tended to be unstable and not always significant. This lack of robustness might be linked to the fact that in Latin America, independent regulators are still the exception rather than the rule (less than 20 percent of sectors have an independent regulator) and that it is difficult to measure actual independence, so no clear effect can be observed on that dimension. Still, the principle stands that regulatory institutions should be given as much autonomy as possible—managerially, operationally, financially, and in terms of security of employment. The closer the regulatory agency is to the executive branch, the weaker its filtering role is.

The type of regulation also affects the probability of renegotiation, as the theory predicts, through risk allocation. Rate-of-return regulation lowers the cost of capital as well as the probability of renegotiation because the costs of potential adverse events are borne by government—in contrast to price-cap regulation, in which risk is borne by the operator and is more susceptible to shocks, as when adverse events might trigger a demand to renegotiate by an operator seeking to restore financial equilibrium. This effect is quite important because more than three-quarters of the concessions in Latin America and the Caribbean are regulated using price-cap regulation, and the region has a rather volatile economic environment.

Role of Concession Design

Concession design also matters a lot, especially award criteria. Awarding contracts based on the lowest tariff rather than the highest transfer fee significantly increases the probability of renegotiation. First, tariffs are a weak anchor for a concession. They are subject to constant revision, and it is foolish to think that they will be maintained for the duration of a concession using the accorded adjustments. Second, such award criteria impose little lock-in or sunk commitment on operators. Unlike with transfer fees, operators do not have to pay anything up front, so their leverage is much stronger, and they can walk out early with little to lose. Finally, minimum tariffs might be viewed as a proxy for tariff adequacy. Their use as award criteria can lead to the bidding of inadequate tariffs and so prompt requests for renegotiation.

Nationality of the concessionaire refers to affiliation and proximity to government and implies higher possibility of capture and higher success in seeking renegotiation. Again, once players anticipate renegotiation, the game changes strategically. The objective is to secure the concession and renegotiate for better terms. That might induce risky offers and lead to the selection not of the most efficient operator but the one most skilled in renegotiation or with higher affiliation.

Investment obligations can also affect renegotiation. These refer to regulating by means as opposed to regulating by objectives. Because the investments need to be evaluated, monitored, and accounted for, permanent conflict exists in determining and agreeing on what counts as investments (for example, firms often argue that severance payments should count as investments), the amounts of investments, prices paid or transfer fees used, and so on. That leads to protracted negotiations and can lead to renegotiation. In principle the implications are clear: no investment obligations should be required, just requirements to achieve a number of outcome targets (performance measures). That approach avoids the problem of measuring investment, manipulation of transfer fees, and proper use of investment.

One statistic already mentioned that supports these findings is the low incidence of renegotiation (about 8 percent) for concessions awarded by bilateral negotiations. Renegotiation is far more likely under competitive bidding for a concession than under direct adjudication. Away from a competitive bidding environment, an operator might secure all the benefits or rents at the start, making renegotiation unnecessary from the operator's perspective.

Most projects awarded through bilateral negotiations in Latin America have been in the energy sector and to a lesser extent the transportation sector. This approach has been less common in the telecommunications and water sectors, as noted above. Many of the contracts in the electricity sector have been generous deals, and the operators have been content to maintain them for the life of the concession. The few that have been renegotiated have been at government insistence. Similar patterns appear for transportation (roads) contracts.

Macroeconomic factors, especially devaluations, also increase the likelihood of renegotiation. Here the implication is clear. Revenues from infrastructure services are collected in domestic currency, but investments tend to be financed with foreign currency. Thus devaluations alter the financial equilibrium of the operator, leading to appropriate requests for renegotiation.

Role of Political Influences

Two political factors appear to affect the probability of renegotiation. One is the extent of corruption. That is, if operators believe that their government counterparts are subject to influence, that will increase the operators' belief that renegotiations and the capture of additional rents are possible. To test for that factor, a probit analysis for renegotiated concessions was performed. The results, shown in appendix 3, support that hypothesis. That is, the corruption variable (the measure of corruption is taken from the data developed by Kaufman, Kraay, and Zoido-Lobaton 1999a,b) is strongly significant.[2] These empirical results suggest a negative correlation between the level of corruption and the quality of enforcement. Moreover, the higher the corruption index is, the higher is the probability of renegotiation—as suggested by Laffont (2001), who develops that hypothesis in a theoretical model and empirically corroborates the theoretical findings using our dataset.

The second political factor affecting the probability of renegotiation is election timing. The implication is that after elections, new administrations tend to reconsider actions taken by previous administrations—either because they have new priorities and a need to change contract terms accordingly, or because of politically motivated objectives. A typical example is when a new administration belongs to a different political party than the previous one and begins to terminate agreements secured by the previous one to politically undermine it. Or a new major gets elected who does not share in the fiscal benefits of a concession yet is supposed to grant the agreed-upon tariff increases—suffering their political costs. Many new majors have refused to grant such increases and have sought renegotiation.

To test for possible sectoral effects, similar probit estimates were run for concessions in the water and sanitation sector and for concessions in the

---

2. Similar testing using the corruption index developed by Transparency International shows similar results.

transportation sector. The results—significant coefficients—were generally consistent with those from the integrated analysis. The main effect is the weakening of the significance of the award criteria coefficient. That effect is apparently being picked up by the sector dummy variables where most of the minimum tariff award criteria were used.

7

Policy Implications and Lessons: Guidelines for Optimal Concession Design

This book has documented the high incidence of renegotiation in infrastructure concessions in Latin America and the Caribbean and tested its determinants. Although some renegotiation is desirable and appropriate, the high incidence raises concerns about the region's framework for concessions as well as questions about how the benefits of competitive bidding are allocated. The goal is not to deter efficient, desirable renegotiation, but rather to dissuade opportunistic, strategic renegotiation—and the capture of rents by operators and governments often associated with it.

Aside from the direct welfare effects of misappropriated rents, renegotiation imposes substantial additional costs on regulators when handling renegotiation petitions and cases. This section focuses on the policy implications of the empirical results and interpretations described above, particularly for concession designs and regulatory frameworks.

Shortcomings in Concession Designs and Regulations That Lead to Renegotiation

Opportunistic renegotiation and strategic bidding does not occur in a vacuum or as a fully exogenous event. To a large extent renegotiation—whether initiated by an operator or government—is a strategic and rational response to the concession environment and to the costs and likelihood of renegotiation success. The friendlier the environment and the less costly such action is, the more likely are claims for renegotiation.

To dissuade frivolous renegotiation and to increase the political cost to governments of unilateral interventions, concession designs and regulatory frameworks matter significantly. Improving concession designs and establishing credible regulations and enforcement will lower the incidence of renegotiation on both sides and improve sector performance. This chapter provides a guided blueprint on how to improve contract and regulatory design, limit renegotiation, and improve sector performance.

Guidelines for Optimal Concession Design

The weaknesses of concession contracts mainly result from their deficient design. Usually they are the result of a hurried process, vested interests, and questionable advice, all combined with the limited experience and resources of governments in designing concessions. Well-designed, well-implemented concessions and related regulations, however, can go a long way toward reducing renegotiation and improving performance.

Although many mistakes have been made with concessions in the past, the experience of more than 15 years makes avoiding such mistakes in the future easy. This section draws on that experience and on this book's empirical analysis, and in doing so, offers a blueprint for concession designs that, if followed, should significantly improve prospects for all concessions, reduce the incidence of renegotiation, and improve sector and economic performance.

Legal Grounding of the Regulatory Framework

The importance of regulation with the strongest possible legal grounding cannot be emphasized enough. Time after time attempts have been made, particularly by incoming administrations, to question existing concessions and to dismantle regulatory setups by previous administrations—often for political rather than technical reasons. Such efforts significantly increase regulatory risk, translating into higher tariffs or lower transfer values. Argentina (water), Bolivia (various sectors), Brazil (water, electricity), Panama (electricity), and Peru (various sectors) are among the countries in which such outcomes have occurred, interfering with budgets, salary scales, and the like.

For example, in Minas Gerais, Brazil, a new governor reversed a contractual agreement that gave operating control of electricity distribution companies to new minority foreign owners who had purchased 33 percent of the distribution companies' shares. Similarly, new mayors in other Brazilian municipalities have contested the concession terms of water and other companies. Such interference argues for the creation of regulatory frameworks and agencies in legislation rather than administrative procedures or presidential decrees. Laws are much harder to overturn or modify than decrees and contracts (Guasch and Spiller 1999).

Addressing Incentives of Financial Advisers

The role and potential impact of financial advisers and investment banks hired to implement concession transactions cannot be downplayed. Often they are the ones designing or advising on the concession. Careful attention must be paid to the incentives in their contract arrangements to take concessions to the point of sale. Often their success (which is linked to their fees or commissions) is measured in a number of ways, including the number of prequalifying and bidding firms for the contract, the winning amount (or minimum tariff) for the contract, and the amount of committed investment secured in the contract. The adviser's response to those objectives is often to make the contract and terms as attractive to investors as possible, even if it is detrimental to long-term efficiency and sector performance, or if it is likely to induce subsequent conflicts.

Those objectives may or may not be stated by the government or grantee of the concession. In any event, the government should be aware of the implications of those objectives and of the incentives of advisers to maximize success.

Sector Restructuring Prior to a Concession

Sector restructuring prior to a concession provides a golden—and unique—opportunity to shape market structure, facilitate competition, and ease the regulatory burden. Once a firm has been privatized, property rights have been adjudicated. At that point any efforts to break up privatized companies using antitrust arguments will be difficult and time consuming.

The Process for Awarding Concessions and Award Criteria

The process of awarding concessions involves a two-stage decision. First, concessions can be awarded directly or competitively. Second, when the concession is awarded competitively, the decision involves selecting the criteria for awarding the concession among the various interested bidders.

Direct adjudication and bilateral negotiation to award concession contracts should be avoided except in exceptional circumstances—such as when a concession has only one candidate. The norm should be to award concessions through competitive processes: meaning, auctions undertaken in the most transparent possible manner (see also Klein 1998d).

As noted, the data collected show that renegotiation was much less likely for concessions granted through bilateral negotiation, but that is likely because available rents were captured through the initial negotiation, reducing the need for opportunistic behavior after the concession award.

A variety of criteria—the competitive factors that interested operators bid on—have been used to allocate concessions in auction settings. The most common are minimum tariff, minimum duration of concession, minimum subsidy, maximum amount offered for the rights to operate the concession, largest investment value, minimum total revenue, largest number of retained workers, and "best" overall proposal. Often a combination of these criteria is used. The most common criteria, particularly in the water sector and toll roads, have been awarding the concession on the basis of either the lowest tariff or a points system combining a technical evaluation and the proposed tariff.

In principle the use of multiple criteria—even with a well-specified scoring formula—is not desirable, because it tends to lack transparency and is very susceptible to manipulation, corruption, and the contesting of the award by the losers, inducing delays and protracted conflict. Although the use of a single criterion should be the norm, not all criteria are equally desirable. Choosing well is crucial, because that single criterion determines how the operator is chosen, and the idea is to choose the "best" operator.

Although adaptation to specific settings and needs is possible, general principles should rule the choice. The criterion should be sufficiently robust to account for the intrinsic uncertainty of a concession that is granted for a very long period. Using a criterion that is likely to be modified in the near future, such as tariffs, is often senseless. The two most common criteria, the lowest tariff or a points system combining a technical evaluation and the proposed tariff, are deficient and should be avoided. Technical proposals are almost useless for any contract that is going to last for 25–30 years and are subject to manipulation and arbitrary decisions, because the evaluation can be highly subjective. No concessionaire is going to follow its original technical proposal for more than six months, and indeed, no government should require it.[1]

---

1. For additional information and a lucid exposition on bidding for concessions and the impact of contract design see Klein (1998a,b,c).

Tariffs are "soft" anchors for concession awarding. They are vulnerable, because they constitute a parameter that, at least every so often, automatically appears at the table for modifications and review, even in the best of circumstances, and at that opportunity if not before, it can be subject to modifications, compensation, and rent extraction. Tariff bids have the major disadvantage that the winning tariff will almost always be less than the long-run marginal cost of providing the service, and they are likely to be changed very quickly—mostly through renegotiation or review. This change can be avoided only if the concession specifies a lease payment for existing assets that is carefully calculated to reflect their value under the concession.

In practice, this specification is all but impossible to achieve. As a consequence, some or most investment required to serve additional customers will be unprofitable for the concessionaire, so that problems in ensuring the concessionaire meets its service targets may be constant. Furthermore, the likelihood is strong (and in fact has been the case) that one or more parties may bid a rather low tariff as a "loss leader," with the objective of securing the concession and recouping any short-term losses by renegotiating a tariff increase at the first possible opportunity.

This strategy will be particularly likely if the concessionaire is able to move from an initial tariff to the new one immediately without requiring a phased adjustment averaged over several years. A variant of this strategy was apparently adopted by at least one of the winning bidders for the large water concessions in Manila (the Philippines), and a good case for that could be made in the water concession in the Province of Buenos Aires. Finally, minimum tariff criteria have little "lock-in" effect. Because winning firms do not pay anything at the transfer of the concession, they have little to lose if they were to walk away from the concession if, say, petitions for renegotiation of contract were to be denied by the government.

The salient option to award a concession that minimizes those problems is first to establish an appropriate level and structure of tariffs before a concession is awarded, together with clear rules for tariff readjustment and revision. The concession should then be awarded to the qualified bidder willing to pay the highest initial payment for a specified concession fee or the highest concession fee for a fixed initial payment. In the event of a negative concession, which is one that is not financially viable (such as some toll roads), the concession should be awarded to the qualified bidder willing to accept the lowest subsidy, given a specified toll fee. Qualification conditions should generally relate to the financial capacity of the bidder and to relevant indicators of experience and technical capability. These conditions should be unambiguous and capable of being answered with a simple "yes or no" to avoid disputes.

Any concession fee is effectively a lease payment for the right to use existing assets, plus the right to serve new customers. It may be paid as some combination of a lump sum at the beginning of the contract and an annual fee over the life of the concession. The higher the initial payment, the larger the risk will be from the perspective of the concessionaire. Because potential bidders will probably apply a higher discount rate to payments made throughout the life of the contract than the government would, the net present value of the concession fee to the government is likely to be higher if it is structured as an annual payment, which also has a tax advantage. Indeed, an annual payment could be considered in some special circumstances, if a grace period of two to three years is given at the beginning of the contract when the cash flow of the concessionaire is likely to be negative because of the need to finance heavy investments, particularly in the water sector.

Moreover, structuring that lease payment as a flow of payments over the life of the concession, rather than a single lump-sum payment at the beginning of the concession, facilitates new governments buying into the concession arrangement, because they will also benefit from the concession not including any tax revenues. Often, after an election, when new governments take over, particularly of opposite parties, they have a tendency to question the previous concessioning arrangements and to create obstacles or slow down compliance with agreed-upon tariff increases, mostly for political reasons and because the new governments do not get any direct financial benefit. Structuring the lease payment over the length of the concession will ameliorate that problem.

The annual concession fee (such as in the water and sanitation sector) is usually structured as a percentage of either bills or receipts. Bidders will always prefer it to be a share of receipts, because this arrangement transfers a part of the risk of nonpayment to the government. To induce increased payment compliance, however, linking the concession fee to a percentage of bills is preferable. In the long run, the difference is probably not important, because any concessionaire will want to get the level of nonpayment to less than 5 percent within three or four years. The case for linking the annual concession fee to revenues is not strong, however, when it is viewed as a lease payment for existing assets. A better alternative would be to determine the annual fee as a fixed sum that is linked to the average tariff, for example, it would be equivalent to the average tariff for x million units of service, where x is either specified or is the outcome of the bidding process.

Structuring the annual concession fee in this way would reinforce the incentive to increase revenues by serving new customers. The following points summarize the awards process:

- The process should be in two stages: the first to prequalify interested parties on the basis of experience and the technical proposal, if applicable, and the second to solicit bids from the prequalified bidders using a single criterion for selection.
- Prequalification should set up eligibility procedures that have strong technical and financial criteria (see table 7.1 for examples).
- The winning bid should be selected solely on the basis of the financial proposals (single criteria, highest canon, or fee) submitted by bidders who have met the technical qualifications, which may include a requirement to submit a technical proposal for meeting the requirements of the contract.
- The financial proposals, or second-stage bidding, should normally be specified in terms of the highest annual canon as a percentage of gross invoices to be paid by the concessionaire (perhaps after a suitable grace period) on the basis of a defined combination of tariffs, initial payment, and assumption of debt.

Implementation of an Optimal Concession Award Criteria

The awarding of a concession should be established using the two stages described earlier. At the second stage, the salient choices for concession award criteria, based on efficiency, incentives, and effectiveness against renegotiation, should be either an annuity payment—canon—or the LPVR when appropriate (see below). The following describes these two criteria in greater detail.

Optimal Transfer Fee—Canon-Based Concession Awarding Criteria

During the second stage, the awarding criteria should be based on the maximum amount for the rights to operate the concession, having established a duration commensurate with the life of the assets (20–30 years) and having set maximum tariffs and regulatory regime as price cap or rate of return. The operator submitting the highest amount obtains the concession. That amount of money is placed into an interest-accumulating trust, which could be invested in risk-free assets, to be disbursed to the government in annual amounts throughout the life of the concession. Even though

Table 7.1 *Examples of Prequalification Criteria in Private Infrastructure Concession and Transactions*

Sector	Country	Transaction	Prequalification procedure	Technical criteria	Financial criteria
Electricity	Peru	Lima electricity distribution privatization	Qualification at time of bidding; bidders must exceed a score of 80 percent against six weighted quantitative technical and financial criteria	Customers and energy sales per worker, total customers, and energy sales	Minimum total value of assets and net worth
Electricity	Argentina	Electricity distribution concessions	A guarantee to carry out the bidding process required of bidders at the time of prequalification	Consortia to include qualified operator with minimum experience and ownership in consortium	Minimum asset value of bidding companies; proven increase of at least 10 percent in asset value in three years prior to bidding
Natural gas	Mexico	Concessioning of distribution	Registration of interested bidders and meetings between regulator and prospective bidders to clarify information prior to technical bids; small registration fee	Documentation of technical and administrative capacity	Documentation of financial capacity

Transportation	Mexico	Concessioning of rail freight lines	Registration through written statement of interest; authorization of registered parties by the Ministry of Communications and Transportation based on uniform criteria	Demonstrated legal, technical, and administrative capacity	Demonstrated financial capacity
Transportation	Hungary	BOT for toll road	Invitations for prequalification based on approved preliminary design plans evaluated by expert assessment committee	Capacity of bidders to design, build, maintain, and operate toll road	Capacity of bidders to finance road without state aid
Water	Argentina	Buenos Aires concession	US$30,000 fee for prequalification documents	Minimum population of largest city and aggregate population served by bidder	Minimum requirements for total annual billing and net share capital; consortium share-holding distribution regime
Water	Bolivia	La Paz concession	Qualification process to take place at same time as economic bids presented	Consortia must include water operator with minimum experience and extent of service	Minimum net worth and maximum debt-to-equity ratio of operator

Source: Kerf and others (1998).

the first payment could be larger than the rest, it should not exceed 15 percent of the total amount. Any government could borrow against these payments, but only for the disbursements matching its elected period.

This scheme has three attractive features. First, it uses a nonsoft criterion to award the concession, which is more difficult to renegotiate and is consistent with the transfer for the use of the existing assets and the right to operate the concession. Second, by forcing the operator to pay a single amount up front, it generates a lock-in effect, increases the commitment of the operator, and grants increased leverage to the government in the event of the operator's performance noncompliance. Third, it provides for increased ownership (of the concession decision) for future governments, because they will also benefit from annual payments.

This component has a drawback, compared with a scheme in which an operator makes annual payments, in the sense that it is financially more expensive, because the amounts of funds needed at the start are clearly greater than in a scheme with a simple canon, paid annually by the operator. Arguably, however, the benefits of increased commitment are bound to be greater than these increased financial costs.

Least Present Value of Revenues

An interesting alternative developed by Engel, Fischer, and Galetovic (1998, 2000) for certain types of concessions is the use of the LPVR as the criterion to allocate concessions. Interested operators bid on the present value of total revenue to be received, and the one submitting the lowest value gains the concession. Once that LPVR is received, the concession ends. The government sets up maximum tariffs and a rate of discount that can be fixed or variable.

This scheme has multiple advantages. Perhaps the most important is that it preempts renegotiation and rent seeking by opportunistic operators. This advantage is most important because renegotiation of concession contracts is pervasive. Almost 50 percent of all concession contracts are renegotiated within three years of the award of the concession, and at least half of the operators are opportunistic to the detriment of the users of the service. Another advantage is the automatic compensation the operator receives if factors such as demand and tariffs adversely affect revenues. The operator can then run the concession for additional years until the agreed-upon LPVR is secured. Thus it preempts needs and requests by operators for demand or traffic guarantees, with their corresponding fiscal implications. In addition, it provides clear and transparent compensation (the residual value of the LPVR) in the event of the need to terminate the contract. In the event of a significant change, say, a request from the government for more investment, that amount can be tagged to the original LPVR bid as the appropriate compensation.

Other advantages are that it provides incentives to operate at optimal costs because any gains are fully captured by the operator, weakens incentives to submit frivolous offers, and lessens the need to evaluate and forecast demand, thereby reducing preparation of bid costs. In addition, it facilitates oversight by regulators and considerably limits regulator's discretion, because oversight is basically limited to assessing and accounting for the flow of revenues. It also lessens incentives to request non-ordinary tariff increases, and, in the event of cancellation of the concession, it facilitates settlement structure because the salient parameter for compensation is the remainder (yet uncollected) of the LPVR. Perhaps the main disadvantages are, first, that the length of the concession is uncertain, which can affect financing, and second, that there is a need for an agreement on the proper discount rate.

When to Select the Transfer Fee or the LPVR Criteria to Award Concessions

Which one of these two should be selected depends on the characteristics of the concession. The key characteristic is whether the quality of service provided by the concessionaire has a strong effect on demand or not. Because the LPVR, in fact, protects the operator against changes in demand, it is appropriate only for settings in which the concessionaire can do little to influence demand and in which objective quality standards can be set, measured, and enforced. Typical settings, then, are roads and highways, landing strips in airports, water reservoirs, and so on. The LPVR criteria have rarely been used, apparently because of opposition by private sector operators, because they take away opportunities for rent-seeking renegotiations. Only four highway concessions have been awarded using these criteria, one in Chile and three in Peru. Alternatively, for settings in which the operator can significantly influence demand through the provision and quality of service, LPVR criteria are not appropriate, and the annuity canon should be used. Typical settings for the latter are water and sanitation concessions, port concessions, network concessions, and so on.

Financial Equilibrium Clauses for the Operation of the Concession in the Concession Contract

Quite often concession contracts or regulatory frameworks, when ordinary or extraordinary tariff reviews are called for, state or make reference to the principle of adjusting variables to secure the financial equilibrium of the concession, usually in a forward-looking manner (for related regulatory processes and instruments with illustrations in Latin America, see Green and Rodriguez-Pardina 1999 for all sectors and Benitez and others 2002 for telecommunications). Although, in principle, this approach is appropriate and consistent with the spirit of regulation, care should be exercised in how it is stated. Broad and sweeping statements without reference points are undesirable and often have been the source of conflicts and inefficiencies. Such clauses should not guarantee the financial equilibrium without making reference to efficient operation and preserving the sanctity of the bid. The risk of an opportunistic bid should be fully borne by the operator.

Similarly, financial equilibrium clauses should specify the capital base on which the firm is allowed to earn a fair return. The capital base ought not necessarily include the transfer fee when the concession was awarded by that criterion. This argument is often key for renegotiation and also for the tariff review process. For if the whole transfer fee is allowed to enter into the capital base, it distorts the competitive bidding and reduces value to the country. It then becomes more like a loan to the country—to be repaid through higher tariffs—than a purchase price indicative of superior efficiency. Thus, on any amount paid, the firm would be allowed to earn a fair rate of return, and that result is not the essence of competitive bidding. The capital base should be linked to the book value of the assets, rather than to the transfer fee. Similarly, accumulated profits should not be allowed to be part of the capital base, a common problem in Latin American and Caribbean countries, where it has been allowed. When they are invested, under the appropriate guidelines, then they ought to enter into the capital base.

Another element that needs to be very clearly stated in the financial equilibrium clause of the contract is the period of application. The period of application refers to the period of time over which the financial equilibrium is evaluated, and in principle it could range from one year to the life of the concession. Both of those extreme points are inappropriate; a three- to five-year period seems more appropriate. If that period is not clearly stated, operators will choose the shortest period when the financial results have been deficient, and the longest period when the financial results are very good. The choice of the relevant period has been a source of conflict when it was not properly specified. Finally, the principle of financial equilibrium should be an ex ante consideration and not ex post market outcome, in the sense that it should not bail the operator out for adverse realizations of normal commercial risk.

Renegotiation Clauses and Triggers for Renegotiation

The intrinsic nature of the subject of concessions contracts in infrastructure is bound to make any contract incomplete. And renegotiation can be an efficient—albeit second best—instrument to address that issue, so it should not be ruled out on principle, but it indeed can be framed to dissuade frivolous claims and support the valid ones. The concession contract should address as clearly as possible (a) events that would trigger tariff adjustments and the extent of the adjustments, and (b) events that would trigger a renegotiation of the contract with guidelines about the process and outcomes of the renegotiation.

The principle is that small changes that affect the financial equilibrium of the firm and that are not controlled by the firm should not require adjustments, but large ones may. Renegotiations should be undertaken in the most transparent manner as possible, preferably by appointing a neutral and professional commission to review the claim and advise on the outcome in a process that is as open as possible.

Sanctity of the Bid

When facing petitions for renegotiation, the sanctity of the bid contract must be upheld. The operator should be held accountable for its submitted bid. The financial equation set by the winning bid should always be the reference point, and the financial equilibrium behind that bid should be restored in the event of renegotiation or adjustment. Renegotiation should not be used to correct for mistakes in bidding or for overly risky or aggressive bids—another reason for the superiority and desirability of transfer fees over minimum tariffs as award criteria for concession awards.

Concession Length and Financing

The combination of long-lived assets and a high degree of specificity has particularly important consequences for the length of the concession contract. If the residual value of an asset at the end of a concession period is highly uncertain, concessionaires will tend to write off any assets acquired during the concession over the remaining term. Therefore, if this term is short and concessionaires must fund investment in those long-lived assets, they might demand substantial subsidies in exchange for the guarantee of a given level of service. The effect of a shorter contract can be mitigated if assets are acquired at less than the replacement cost (that is, used assets) and if the government promises to repurchase them at a fair market value should the concession be lost to the investor. Nevertheless, this situation need not mean that short-term concessioning is not viable or that it is less attractive than long-term concessioning.

In fact, each approach has advantages and disadvantages. Short-term concessioning allows more frequent competition and, therefore, maximizes the incentive to increase efficiency. An example of a short concession is the distribution and transmission in the power sector in Argentina. The regulatory agency usually fixes the tariffs for five years. At the end of this period, an international bid is called for the sale of the control package of the concessionaire. The incumbent puts his "reserve price" into a sealed envelope. Bids are accepted from all interested parties. If the incumbent is the highest bidder, it keeps the concession with no payment. If the incumbent is outbid, it receives the highest bid (net of any debt to the state), and the winning bidder gets the concession. Shorter-term concession contracts coupled with competitive rollovers at the end of a contract can be a powerful efficiency-inducing device, as long as the firm is compensated for incurred investments.

Long-term concessioning not only minimizes some of this incentive but also fosters a relationship that is more akin to that of regulator and regulated than a true business contract. Long-term concessioning, however, also maximizes the opportunities for shifting responsibility to the private sector. It encourages more innovation and cost-efficiency than a short-term contract. Which of these factors will weigh more heavily with policymakers will depend on the specific local circumstances. For example, on a network in which the assets have been recently renewed, the attraction of frequent competition might outweigh the benefits of long-term concessioning. For parts of the network in which track and rolling stock are in urgent need of renewal, a long concession period might be attractive.

Investment Commitments

Although obligations for investment commitments have been a fixture in practically all concession contracts, they should be avoided as much as possible and replaced by specific outcomes, such as the building of a new water treatment plant, access road, and so forth when applicable, and clear technical and quality specifications should be used or, even better, when possible, outcome indicators, such as coverage rates, quality standards, or technical achievements, should be specified. A timing schedule should accompany those specifications, gradually increasing those targets over the life of the concessions. The targets should be easy to measure, and a description of how they will be measured should be included. Governments have found requesting investment amounts in contracts to be politically attractive, because the success of investments is associated with significant improvements in sector performance, new jobs created, and increased economic activities.

Investments are just a means to secure the ultimate objective, improve sector performance, increase coverage, and achieve related objectives, but as discussed earlier, the measurement of realized investments and assessment of transfer prices has been, is, and will be a continuing source of conflicts and a precursor to renegotiations. As an illustration of the issue, in the El Callao-Peru airport concession, the concessionaire is claiming investments of about US$60 million toward meeting a required first target of US$80 million by August 4, while the regulator, OSITRAN, is only allowing US$27 million of those US$60 million. To avoid that problem, stating directly the outcomes those investments ought to produce is much better and more efficient. That directness is usually easy to measure and oversee and is nonconflictive. To link outcomes and investments, common practice should be to request from the concessionaire, after the concession is awarded, a program or action plan about how the operator intends to secure those scheduled targets and the involved associated amounts of investments that will be required, even though such action plans are no more than indicative and nonbinding, and essentially serve to ensure consistency and feasibility in achieving those targets over time.

Determining Future Tariffs

The common and appropriate structure of tariff setting—under a price-cap regime, which has been the salient choice in developing countries—is that a very simple initial tariff structure is established that applies for the first five years of the contract, subject to annual readjustment for inflation in a given month of each year. Tariff revisions should normally occur at five-year intervals and must follow a formula that applies to the average tariff that is billed by the concessionaire, but the circumstances under which an extraordinary tariff revision is permitted should be narrowly defined.

Then the issue is the process and guidelines for adjusting the tariffs at the five-year interval. An important issue concerns the extent of regulatory discretion in the revision of tariffs at, say, five-year intervals under a price-cap regime. Much of the experience and literature on the subject assumes that tariffs will be set on a forward-looking basis under which the regulator attempts to estimate the level of revenues—and, hence, tariffs—that will be required to cover the operating and depreciation costs of an efficient operator together with a return on capital on the regulatory asset base. This approach allows a large degree of discretion to the regulator in fixing many of the critical parameters that enter into the calculation—for example, the cost of capital, improvements in operating efficiency, and the cost of investment programs.

Implementing a major revision of tariffs is a severe test for any regulatory agency, especially when it has limited past experience and guidelines to rely upon. Thus, investors may have reasonable reservations about how the regulatory discretion will be used, which will be reflected in a higher premium for regulatory uncertainty. They may, therefore, strongly prefer the alternative of relying upon a backward-looking formula for revising tariffs. Under this arrangement, the concession contract would specify—in more or less detail—a method of determining the average tariff for the next period using data on costs, assets, and so forth at the end of the previous period. Some discretion is possible by allowing the regulator to determine the value of x in the usual RPI-x readjustment formula, for price-cap regulated concessions, where RPI stands for the rate of price index increases.

In the longer term, backward-looking mechanisms for price revision will come to be seen as excessively rigid. Furthermore, pressure to increase the degree of regulatory discretion to reflect changes in circumstances and political priorities will be brought to bear. This aspect is but one part of the broader reality that concession contracts are never static, but are subject to a continuous process of renegotiation. Building up a stock of confidence and case-law must come first, however, because they give concessionaires a reasonable basis for believing that they will be treated reasonably by the regulators in the exercise of their discretionary powers. The key contract provisions about tariff revisions should include the following:

- Arrangements and criteria for the readjustment and revision of tariffs should be clear.
- Readjustments should occur annually (or more frequently when permitted by law) in March or April based on inflation to the end of December of the previous year.
- Tariffs should normally be revised at intervals of five years using a predefined formula based on the reasonable costs of providing the service including a return on assets employed in providing the service. This return on assets is calculated according to the capital asset pricing model with a provision to implement revised tariffs gradually over the following five years.
- Extraordinary revisions of tariffs should be permitted only in clearly defined circumstances, such as changes in the rates or calculation of

specific taxes and allowed costs and should not cover the normal commercial risks of providing the service such as changes in the cost of labor or operational inputs.

- Frivolous and opportunistic renegotiation of tariffs and terms should be strongly discouraged via specific penalties in the event of a ruling by neutral body of such motivation.

Regulatory Structure: Rate of Return Versus Price Caps

When designing a concession contract, a choice needs to be made regarding the regulatory regime. The two salient choices are rate-of-return regulation and price-cap regulation. Under a rate-of-return regulation, the firm's returns can be adjusted each year, and that readjustment will keep the rate of return roughly constant. Thus investments in the firm are subject to little risk, particularly the market-related risk that investors worry about. If returns in the market as a whole rise, the regulated utility's returns will not rise much (although they can rise a little in the period before the regulator requires a price cut). In the event of a market downturn, the firm's profits will not fall below the contractually agreed-upon target set for long. The regulator will adjust tariffs to induce the agreed-upon rate of return. So, firms subject to rate-of-return regulation tend to have a lower than average cost of capital.

Price-cap regulation has a different effect. In the short run, the regulator does not set a target rate of return. Therefore, profits from the regulated firm can vary from period to period and are free to vary with the returns on the market. Because, on average, firms subject to price caps are suppose to be in financial equilibrium, their average profits or returns are subject to less risk than other nonregulated firms. The risk that affects a firm's cost of capital can be measured by a parameter, called the firm's beta, which measures the relative risk of the firm's equity compared to the market as a whole (and its value depends on the type of regulation used, when that is appropriate). The higher the beta, the higher the riskiness of the investment or project.

Betas for infrastructure firms or projects are lower than 1, an average for all firms (table 7.2). But firms subject to price-cap regulation have higher betas than firms subject to rate-of-return regulation. This fact has been shown by, among others, Alexander, Estache, and Oliveri (2001) and Alexander, Mayer, and Weeds (1996), who show that price caps are indeed associated with higher cost of capital than rate-of-return regulation both for utilities and transportation operations. Thus, investors, not surprisingly, will demand a higher return for investment in a firm subject to price-cap regulation. Establishing the values for each of these items is relatively straightforward

Table 7.2 *Average Infrastructure Firm Betas, by Country, Sector, and Type of Regulation, 1990s*

Country	Electricity		Gas		Combined gas and electricity		Water		Telecommunications	
	Regulation	Beta	Regulation	Beta	Regulation	Beta	Regulation	Beta	Regulation	Beta
Canada	—	—	—	—	ROR	0.25	—	—	ROR	0.31
Japan	ROR	0.43	—	—	—	—	—	—	ROR	0.62
Sweden	—	—	—	—	—	—	—	—	Price cap	0.50
United Kingdom	—	—	Price cap	0.84	—	—	Price cap	0.67	Price cap	0.87
United States	ROR	0.30	ROR	0.20	ROR	0.25	ROR	0.29	Price cap (AT&T)	0.72
									ROR (others)	0.52

— Not available.
ROR Rate of return.
Source: Alexander, Mayer, and Weeds (1996).

when developed capital markets exist and companies are quoted on a stock exchange. Approximations must be used in most developing countries. The average asset beta in infrastructure (which accounts for the leverage in the capital structure of the projects) is around 0.7 for high-powered incentive regimes, such as price-cap regulation and around 0.3 for low-powered incentive regimes such as rate-of-return regulation. Both of them are below 1, which is the average beta for the market as a whole.

Latin American countries adopted the price-cap regime with a vengeance. Unfortunately, they merely swallowed rather than digested the concept, not accounting for its full range of implications. The problems the region has experienced with the reform program in infrastructure and with the adoption of price caps are, to some extent, the result of this eagerness to adopt a concept in theory rather than in practice, without accounting for its full implications.

The two types of regulatory regimes have tradeoffs. A price cap is a high-power mechanism providing incentives for securing efficiency gains, at least between tariff reviews, and is low maintenance in the sense that it does not require, at least between tariff reviews, a great deal of information about the firm's operations. Yet price-cap regimes induce a higher cost of capital, as a result of their inherent riskiness. Rate-of-return regulation is a lower power incentive mechanism, does not provide for strong incentives to reduce costs, requires a much higher information level for the regulator, but induces lower cost of capital because its associated risk is lower.

In practice both regimes tend to converge, and the level of convergence depends on the frequency of tariff reviews. The shorter the period between tariff reviews, the higher the convergence. Table 7.3 illustrates that price caps strongly increase the probability of renegotiation, and that effect brings convergence even closer, because the outcomes of the renegotiation process often include increasing the number of cost components with an automatic pass-through to tariffs, toward a hybrid regime. Moreover given that renegotiation happens, on average, only two years after the time of award, the efficiency effects of a price-cap regime are wasted. As a risk-mitigation strategy aiming at offsetting the increase in the cost of capital, the request, as part of the renegotiation, for automatic pass-through rules for as many categories as possible was thus a rational strategy for the operators. It was, of course, not the only instrument, and in many instances, the renegotiations were aimed at increasing the rate of return to keep it consistent with the increasing cost of capital or with oversights at the bidding stage. Thus, slowing down investment, reducing service obligations, or increasing direct or indirect subsidies were all addressed as part of the renegotiations, in

Table 7.3 *Incidence of Renegotiated Concession Contracts According to Sectors and Characteristics*
(percent)

Regulatory regime	All infrastructure sectors	Transportation	Water and sanitation
Incidence of renegotiation	30.0	54.7	75.4
With price cap	42.1	55.1	88.0
With rate of return	12.9	38.1	14.3
With hybrid regime[a]	24.4	46.2	39.6

a. Hybrid regimes are defined when, under a regime of price caps, a large number of costs components are allowed automatic pass-through into tariff adjustments. The numbers for the hybrid regimes are subjective, because information used to determine the classification was incomplete.
Source: Author's calculations.

particular in the water and transportation sectors. This led to the common outcome of most renegotiations of a decrease in the level and pace of investments.

The evidence available on price caps as a source of concern for the operators comes, not surprisingly, from the preference for less risky regulatory regimes as shown by the changes brought by renegotiation. As already mentioned, renegotiation tends to lead to a transformation of most price caps into hybrid regimes, and delegitimizes the price-cap regime, both on the grounds of the speed of change of the agreed-upon terms and of the outcome. This delegitimization, in turn, suggests that if a cost-plus regime had been adopted to begin with, renegotiation may have been reduced. The way the price caps, and more generally reforms, were handled in practice raises some frustrating questions. Would a regime that is less incentive-based have resulted in more and better investment? Had the region created earlier, stronger, and better regulatory institutions, would the outcomes have been better? Was the problem the choice of the regulatory regime, or are we trying to blame everything on one of many factors that contributed to the high renegotiation rates? Finally, could the high incidence of renegotiation have been avoided?

The answers to most of these questions boil down to an understanding of how price caps and cost of capital interact in high-risk, weak-governance environments. Weak regulatory capacity and weak government commitment to improve that capacity in Latin America led to the fact that price caps alone did not yield the expected benefits for the users. Price caps did provide incentives for operators to secure efficiency gains quickly, but many of these gains were then captured by the governments or firms rather than shared with the users. Users were in fact penalized twice, because these efficiency gains came at the cost of a higher cost of capital and thus higher tariffs to cover that increase—relative to a rate-of-return regime. Compounding the pain inflicted on the users is the fact that renegotiations, generally associated with the adoption of a price-cap regime, tended to delay or bring down investment levels, because firms do not get immediate rewards—through tariff adjustments—on investments. Either the existing tariffs already account for expected investments, or tariffs will be adjusted but only at the next tariff review period, usually a few years down the road.

Ultimately, the easiness and fast renegotiation of contracts—before the usual five-year review— may eventually lead to the adoption of new regimes that will result in fairer tariffs, better access, and stronger commitment to fair returns to investors. This result seems to be happening through the adoption of hybrid regimes, which will retain some of the incentive effects of the price caps while introducing cost-recovery guarantees that may ultimately reduce tariffs, because they will reduce the uncertainty of doing business in the region and, hence, the cost of capital. In sum, what the 1990s Latin American experience shows is that, just as privatization alone (for example, without competition) is associated with few benefits for an economy, price caps alone will not do much for the users.

In light of all that, one could argue that rate-of-return regulation should be favored in developing countries when choosing among regulatory regimes particularly for concessions that require significant amounts of investments, despite the fact that overseeing that regulation effectively requires higher information levels.

Cost of Capital and How It Should Be Determined

Any detailed regulatory mechanism, whether a price cap or rate of return, requires a financial equilibrium of the operation of the concession, that is, the ability to generate enough returns to reward the capital investments with its associated risks. (This section is adapted from Estache and de Rus 2000). That condition implies imputing the cost of capital and then coming up with the tariffs that will generate sufficient returns to cover that cost or rate of return. Thus properly assessing that cost of capital, which is often sector specific, is most important. Governments must also avoid the common practice of overestimating the amount of money or investment that they will receive from privatization because they assume that the cost of capital is much lower than its true cost. In practice, this bias is partially offset by a tendency to underestimate the scope for reducing average operating costs and improving revenue collection.

In consequence, a set of principles must be established to determine the cost of capital to be used in the revision of tariffs. The usual approach is to follow the capital asset pricing model. The cost of capital represents the required rate of return that investors might expect on a project. Because capital has usually two components, equity and debt, the cost of capital can be written as shown below.

> Cost of capital
>
> =
>
> (Required rate of return on debt)
>
> x
>
> (Debt percentage in the project)
>
> +
>
> (Required rate of return on equity)
>
> x
>
> (Equity percentage in the project)

Because interest expense typically is tax deductible, the cost of capital can be calculated either on a before-tax or an after-tax basis. The tax rate that is relevant is the one that applies to project sponsors. One can think about the required rate of return on debt (that is, the borrowing cost) as having a number of risk factors, each of which commands a premium that must be paid to investors for them to bear that particular risk.[2] A very important one is regulatory risk.

Once the operator has to make a large commitment of resources—either in purchasing the right to use existing assets or through investments in new fixed assets—it will be concerned by the risk of effective expropriation as a consequence of changes in regulations, tariffs, or contract terms, which prevent it from earning an adequate return on the capital that it has allocated to the business. The consequence of this regulatory uncertainty is

---

2. The question arises about whether these risk factors are separately priced in financial markets or whether they can be diversified in well-designed international portfolios. The structure and model used here leave open the possibility that such factors may not be priced by allowing them to take on values of zero. For a discussion of factor models see Ross, Westerfield, and Jaffe (1999, pp. 271–88).

that investors will add a substantial premium to the rate of return that they expect to achieve when bidding for concession contracts in infrastructure services. This uncertainty will be reflected both in the value assessed by investors of the existing infrastructure and in the tariff required to sustain investment in expanding infrastructure.

> Required rate of return on debt
> =
> Risk-free borrowing rate for specified time horizon
> +
> Premium for country risk
> +
> Premium for currency risk
> +
> Premium for project or sector risk
> +
> Premium for regulatory risk

Similarly, one can think about the required rate of return on equity investment as being equal to a risk-free rate plus a premium for the higher risk faced by equity relative to debt, as well as all four risk factors above. The equity risk premium is a function of how risky a specific sectoral investment is relative to equity markets overall. This factor is the beta (see Alexander, Estache, and Oliveri 2001). Thus, the following applies.

> Required rate of return on equity
> =
> Risk-free borrowing rate for specified time horizon
> +
> Equity risk premium (adjusted by project beta)
> +
> Premium for country risk
> +
> Premium for currency risk
> +
> Premium for project or sector risk
> +
> Premium for regulatory risk

Although in many cases the risk premiums required would be similar for debt and equity, this situation will not always be the case. For example, regulatory lags in approving pricing decisions may have a greater effect on equity holders, because creditors have a prior claim. This formulation of the required rate of return also allows both parties to evaluate the effects of changing risk premiums and guarantees on the cost of capital.

To measure the overall return that shareholders in a specific project earned on the capital they invested in that project, and then determine if that return is appropriate given the risk they took, one computes the internal rate of return they made on their investment (IRR) and compares it with the cost of equity (C_E) in the country and sector of investment. Box 7.1 illustrates how the cost of equity is defined explicitly and how it is measured.

Box 7.1 *The Cost of Equity*

The cost of equity is a measure of the appropriate return that investors should expect on equity investments in a specific country and sector, given the level of risk of such investments.

The formulas used to estimate the cost of equity (C_E) are usually based on the capital asset pricing model developed by Gordon and Shapiro (1956), which is expressed as follows:

$$C_E = (R_f) + (MRP) * \beta + CRP + SRRP,$$

where

R_f = risk-free rate
MRP = market risk premium
β = sector beta
CRP = country risk premium
$SRRP$ = sector and regulatory risk premium

Each of these parameters corresponds to a level of return necessary to compensate for some specific risks:

- The risk-free rate is the minimum return that can be earned on a risk-free investment. It is generally measured as the average interest rate on the U.S. Treasury bill over a long historical period.
- The market risk premium is the additional return that must be earned on equity investments over risk-free investments to compensate for their additional nondiversifiable risk. It is generally measured as the average excess return on the U.S. stock market (measured using returns on

The volatility of the cost of capital in the Latin American and Caribbean region is a factor in the sustainability of concessions. As an example, table 7.4 shows the variation in the cost of equity by sector in the region. The two cost of equity columns show its average value at the time of the award (initial) and the value in 2001(current). The obvious increase in this cost of capital across sectors corroborates the hypothesis made above, but it understates the actual total cost of capital, because it does not recognize the significant increase in the costs of debt. In the water and transportation sectors, the investment needs were the highest, but at the same time, cost recovery through tariffs was the most politically difficult for obvious social and political reasons. In these two sectors the expected fiscal contribution of the public sector in the form of subsidies for operational or capital expenditures was also expected to be the highest and seldom delivered on.

the S&P500 for instance) above the risk-free rate over a long historical period.

- Beta is a measure of the nondiversifiable risk of stock market investments in a specific industry. It is usually estimated by specialist firms based on many financial, operational, and strategic characteristics of each industry. The market risk premium is multiplied by beta, because investors are compensated only for risks that cannot be diversified by an appropriate portfolio management.
- The country risk premium is a measure of the extra risk taken when investing in a specific country. It is generally measured on the basis of the country's Moody or other credit rating compared to the U.S. rating, comparing the average spread on bonds of that country with equivalent spreads in the United States over a long historical period.
- The sector and regulatory risk premium is a measure of the risk of government noncompliance with agreed-upon regulatory terms or of unilateral changes by government on the regulatory framework. It is generally measured by an index capturing the historical volatility of regulatory changes and noncompliance, and by the degree of independence of the regulatory agency. Often it is also measured by surveying existing and potential operators. It can fall in the range of 2–6 percentage points of the cost of capital.

If the overall return earned by project shareholders on their investment is lower than the cost of equity measured in this way, they would have been better off investing their money in alternative investments given that they earned too little compared to the risk they took.

Table 7.4 *The Cost of Equity in Latin America in the 1990s*
(percent)

Sector	Initial cost of equity	Current cost of equity
Energy	14.0	18.8
Telecommunications	14.0	19.5
Transportation	17.5	21.0
Water and sanitation	15.5	19.0

Source: Foster and others (2003).

Tariff and Revenue Implications of Increased Cost of Capital

Increases in the cost of capital translate into higher required tariffs; lower annual fees, canons, or transfer fees; or higher required subsidies, if applicable. To understand the impact of increases in the cost of capital, the following might help. Suppose a US$100 million dollar project has a 25-year life. An increase in the cost of capital from 15 to 20 percent would require additional payments to investors of about US$5 million per year. The premium on the cost of capital as a result of regulatory uncertainty—as distinct from the country risk—in Latin American countries has been estimated to be 3–7 percent.

Another way to see the impact is that an increase in the cost of capital of 5 percent would imply, when offering a concession, a reduction of about 30 percent in the net present value of the initial payment and the concession fee realized by selling the company. Alternatively, the overall level of tariffs would have to be about 25 percent higher for the first five years of the concession to realize a fixed net present value for the company. Thus, the cost of regulatory uncertainty will be directly reflected in the proceeds that can be realized by awarding private concessions or in the tariffs that must be charged to cover the debts that have accumulated by the existing operators.

The premium for regulatory uncertainty does not disappear rapidly, no matter what steps are taken to establish a better and more reliable regulatory framework. Confidence in regulatory arrangements is built up gradually, decision by decision, and gains from improvements in regulatory oversight will be secured. These gains will come via a reduction in the rate of return required by investors, which will increase the value of existing concessions as well as the prices offered for new concessions. Some of the benefits will accrue to those who take on concessions now, because otherwise they will have little incentive to take the large risks involved.

Under reasonable rules for setting tariffs, however, part of this gain will accrue to customers in the form of lower tariffs for service.

Concession Risks and Their Allocation

A key element of concession design is the identification of associated risks and their proper allocation. The latter has a major impact on the costs of capital and tariff levels. Because concession design aims to establish financial equilibrium for the concessionaire, inadequately assigned risk would raise both. The two principles guiding risk allocation are (a) the party that is responsible or has more control over the risk factor should bear the risk, and (b) the party that is more able to bear the risk (less risk-averse) should be assigned the risk. Under those criteria the major risks and their allocation in a concession are shown in table 7.5.

Valuation of Concession Assets

What clearly should not be used for the value of the concession in the capital base—from which the operator is allowed to earn a fair rate of return—is the value paid at the bidding stage, regardless of depreciation method. Doing that would take away the efficiency-competitive angle of the auction, by allowing a rate of return on whatever price was paid for the concession. Using the depreciated book value of assets (after adjustment for inflation) as the capital base in the calculation of tariffs is standard practice. Furthermore, depreciation periods for most infrastructure assets are much shorter than the physical life of the assets. The effect is a large but unrecognized transfer from current customers to future ones, especially when a utility undertakes a large program of investments. Current capital charges—depreciation and return on capital—are high but these costs fall because the book value of assets after depreciation declines. Thus, even if the real cost of providing infrastructure services is essentially unchanged, the level of tariffs will steadily fall. This trend is both inequitable and inefficient. Future consumers are likely to be richer, so requiring current consumers to make a disproportionate contribution to the cost of infrastructure makes no sense. More important, the decline in tariffs will cause them to fall below the real cost of providing services, and that decline will undermine the incentive of the concessionaire to maintain or replace infrastructure. Sooner or later, tariffs will have to be raised sharply to correct this situation, and that increase may be unpopular and difficult to justify unless systems have visibly deteriorated.

Table 7.5 Identification and Allocation of Risks

What is the risk?	How does it arise?	How should it be allocated?
Design or development risk		
Design defect	Design fault in tender specifications	Public sector to bear risk
	Contractor design fault	Liquidated damages to be paid by contractor; once liquidated damages are exhausted, erosion of project company's returns
Construction risk		
Cost overrun	Within construction consortium's control (inefficient construction practices, and so on)	Contractor to bear risk through fixed-price construction contract plus liquidated damages; once liquidated damages are exhausted, erosion of project company's returns
	Outside construction consortium's control: changes in the overall legal framework (changes of laws, increased taxes, and so on)	Insurer risk if insurance is available; once insurance proceeds are exhausted, erosion of project company's returns
	Outside construction consortium's control: actions of government that specifically affect the project (delays in obtaining approvals or permits, and so on)	Public sector to bear risk
Delay in completion	Within construction consortium's control (lack of coordination of subcontractors, and so on)	Liquidated damages to be paid by contractor; once liquidated damages are exhausted, erosion of project company's returns
	Outside construction consortium's control (an unexpected event, and so on)	Insurer risk, if risk was insured; once insurance proceeds are exhausted, erosion of project company's returns

What is the risk?	How does it arise?	How should it be allocated?
Failure of project to meet performance criteria at completion	Quality shortfall, defects in construction, and so on	Liquidated damages to be paid by contractor; once liquidated damages are exhausted, erosion of project company's returns
Operating cost risk		
Operating cost overruns	Change in practice of operator at project company's request	Project company to bear risk
	Operator failure	Liquidated damages to be paid by operator to the project company; once liquidated damages are exhausted, erosion of project company's returns
Failure or delay in obtaining permissions, consents, and approvals	Public sector discretion	Public authorities to bear risk
Changes in prices of supplies	Increased prices	Allocation of risk to the party best able to control, manage, or bear it (supplier, project company, or users)
Nondelivery of supplies on the part of public authorities	Public sector failure	Public authorities to bear risk
Revenue risk		
Changes in tariffs	In accordance with the terms of the contract (for example, indexation of tariffs leads to reduced demand)	Project company to bear risk
	Government breach of the terms of the contract	Public sector to bear risk

(Table continues on the following page.)

Table 7.5 *(continued)*

What is the risk?	How does it arise?	How should it be allocated?
Changes in demand	Decreased demand	Project company to bear risk
Shortfall in quantity, or shortfall in quality leading to reduced demand	Operator's fault	Liquidated damages to be paid by the operator; once liquidated damages are exhausted, erosion of project company's returns
	Project company's fault	Liquidated damages to be paid by the project company to public authority
Financial risk		
Exchange rates; interest rates	Devaluation of local currency; fluctuations	Project company to bear risk (hedging facilities might be put in place)
Foreign exchange	Nonconvertibility or nontransferability	Public sector to bear risk; in case of contract termination, compensation to be paid by government
Unexpected event risk		
Acts of God	Floods, earthquakes, riots, strikes, and so on	Insurer risk, if risk was insured; otherwise, risk to be borne by project company
Changes in law	Changes in general legal framework (taxes, environmental standards, and so on)	Normally, project company to bear risk (public sector could bear risk when changes are fundamental and completely unforeseeable; for example, switch from free market to central planning)
	Changes in legal or contractual framework directly and specifically affecting the project company	Public sector to bear risk

What is the risk?	How does it arise?	How should it be allocated?
Performance risk		
Political unex-pected event	Breach or cancellation of contract; expropriation, creeping expropriation, failure to obtain or renew approvals	Insurer's risk, if risk was insured; otherwise risk to be borne by public sector; in case of contract termin-ation, compensation to be paid by government
Environmental risk		
Environmental incidents	Operator's fault	Liquidated damages to be paid by the operator; once liquidated damages are exhausted, erosion of project company's returns
	Pre-existing environmental liability	Public sector to bear risk

Source: Kerf and others (1998).

Part of the solution lies in the adoption of more realistic depreciation periods for infrastructure assets. Current depreciation follows conventional tax and accounting rules, but regulators can easily require that capital values for setting tariffs be computed in a more appropriate manner. Relying upon regulatory decisions alone could lead, however, to difficulties in agreeing on the basis for paying compensation at the end of a concession contract or in the event of earlier termination, because such compensation will normally include a payment equal to the un-depreciated value of capital assets. Thus, the basis on which depreciation should be calculated should be clearly specified in concession contracts.

This solution is only partial, because the real problem flows from the fact that the structure of assets and investments of the typical concession will be far from that for an infrastructure operation in some kind of steady growth equilibrium. A better alternative would, therefore, be to rely upon a full-cost-of-service approach that takes into account the replacement value of all of the assets of the concession and allows for the estimated depreciation of these assets over standard periods rather than according to historical accounting conventions. The regulatory asset base would thus be equal to the replacement value of the concession assets and would be quite separate from the book value of such assets.

One merit of this approach is that it would avoid the inconsistent accounting treatment of concession assets. Despite the fact that the concessionaire does not own the assets and cannot mortgage or sell them, they are included in the balance sheet as if they were conventional fixed assets. A clear separation should be made between (a) the assets owned by the concessionaire, and (b) the assets that are used to provide services and should be included in the determination of tariffs. Similar issues apply on asset valuation at the end of the concession when a clause is included allowing for compensation for assets that are not fully depreciated. Box 7.2 illustrates several options to secure that valuation.

Box 7.2 *Measures for Determining Compensation at the Termination of a Concession*

The following are five asset-valuation methods, presented in order of increasing sophistication, that could be used to determine the amount of compensation to be paid to the concessionaire for sunk investments at the termination of the concession.

- *Historical cost.* This approach is the traditional accounting method of valuation for the purpose of financial reporting. It takes the cost of the asset when it was purchased and depreciates it over a certain period. As a measure of current value, it can be misleading because it ignores inflation and thus tends to undervalue assets.
- *Inflation-adjusted historical cost.* Historical cost can be adjusted to take inflation into account by increasing book value according to either a measure of the general inflation rate, such as the consumer price index, or a measure more closely related to the assets involved.
- *Depreciated replacement cost.* An alternative is to consider what it would cost to buy the equivalent asset now or, because similarly degraded second-hand assets may not be readily available, what it would cost to replicate the investment now, less an estimate of the asset's depreciation in value since investment. A problem with the historical cost and depreciated replacement cost is that they do not consider changes in the value of assets brought about by changes in technology.
- *Optimized depreciated replacement cost (ODRC)—or modern-equivalent-asset (MEA) value.* This approach is a refinement of depreciated replacement cost. It is the cost of replacing the asset with the cheapest asset that does the same job (the optimal asset). For example, if a new pipe-making material has been put on the market since the pipes in a water concession were laid, the optimized replacement cost is the cost of replacing the pipes using the new, cheaper material. As before, the cost of the new pipe must be depreciated to account

Informational Requirements Set in the Concession Contract

Effective regulation requires good information about the operations of the regulated firm. Information about costs, revenues, prices, investments, financial data, and realized demand needs to be collected from the opera- tor periodically. Box 7.3 shows the list of information and documents that the operator should provide the regulator annually. The concession con- tract should state, as clearly as possible, the information and its form and frequency that the operating firm must provide to the regulator (see Estache and others 2002 for an exposition of the main issues). The contract should provide the regulator with subpoena powers to coerce the information from the operator in the event of noncooperation plus the right to impose

for its deterioration. ODRC solves the problem of changing technology, but like its predecessors, it has the effect of compensating concessionaires ac- cording to some measure of the cost of investment. Concessionaires could thus be compensated even for making investments that were economically undesirable—that is, investments with benefits that fall short of their costs, even when the costs are as low as possible.

- *Optimized deprival value (ODV)—or market value.* The method of optimized deprival value attempts to take into account value as well as cost: the *ODV* is the minimum of the ODRC and economic value, where economic value is the maximum of the net present value (NPV) of future earnings and disposal value, and disposal value is the amount the asset could be sold for. All to- gether, this implies that

$$ODV = \min [ODRC, \max (NPV \text{ of future earnings, disposal value})].$$

To avoid incentive problems, the estimate of future earnings must be based on an estimated future tariff that is independent of the bids made when the con- cession is re-awarded. In principle, *ODV* accounting may generate compensa- tion payments that give concessionaires the right incentives. Determining the *ODV* of the concessionaire's assets is difficult, however, and requires assess- ments of technology, the concessionaire's expected cash flows, and its cost of capital. The choice of accounting rule must, of course, take into account the prac- ticality, as well as the theoretical advantages of the options. In addition, it should be noted that ODRC and *ODV* subject the concessionaire to certain risks that do not arise with the simpler measures of value. As a result, they may raise the cost of the concessionaire's capital.

Source: Kerf and others (1998).

Box 7.3 *Information Requirements for Operators*

The concession must supply to the regulator the following documents for each service activity:

- Regulatory accounting:
  - Income statement*
  - Balance sheet*
  - Cash flow statement*

- Additional documents:
  - Report of accounting procedures used to prepare the financial statements, with a detailed breakdown of the cost drivers
  - Report of detail transactions with related parties
  - Report containing a detailed explanation of current results and any deviation from the budgetary figures
  - Report of the use of assets and investment plans*
  - Sources of financing of current and future investments
  - Operational statistics*
  - Information about the methodology used to set unregulated prices of monopolistically (or quasi-monopolistically) supplied activities*
  - Auditor's report
  - Declaration of directors' responsibility*
  - Finally, any other information that the concessionaire considers valuable for a better understanding of the information supplied

Note: The elements marked with an asterisk should conform to a specific format provided by the regulator, and the contract should make reference to that format.

---

significant and increasing fines in the event of noncooperation. As obvious as these requirements might seem, plenty of concession contracts have failed to provide those details and rights and have led to a protracted conflict between operator and regulator seeking to obtain relevant information adversely impacting regulatory oversight. Without that explicit mandate legally grounded in the concession contract, the operator, as experience has shown, will be unwilling to provide the relevant information in the proper format. The most common argument used by operators is that information is proprietary and confidential, and their submission of that information might damage their competitive edge.

Regulatory Accounting Norms

Complementing the information requirement issue above, effective regulation requires good data, properly standardized, and even better analysis. Both are problem issues in developing countries. Quite often the concession contract does not specify the format in which the data are to be provided by the regulated firm to the regulatory agency. Proper definition of the different variables and of depreciation and amortization rules, treatment of assets, the accounting methodology (whether to use current cost accounting [CCA] or historical cost accounting , renewal accounting, and so forth), what constitutes a valid investment and what prices are to be used to value investments, and what can be considered to be costs and profits are all lacking. Then, when the regulator requests data and financial information from the firm, it often receives processed data and information that are neither very useful or friendly, rendering the task of regulation even more difficult and increasing the possibility of conflicts and disagreements.

Even when the data and financial information are provided in a friendly format, however, particular care should be taken when analyzing them, because the firm is likely to interpret and manipulate the data to its best advantage, not surprisingly, resulting in imputed rates of return of capital much lower than the reality, to make the case for increase tariff rates. Thus the need for proper regulatory accounting and analysis and the norms should be spelled out in the concession contract (see Campos, Estache, and Trujillo 2003 for a discussion of desirable regulatory accounting structures with application to Argentina's railway sector). Typical questionable practices that are often used—facilitated by the lack of proper regulatory accounting standards—by concessionaires to increase their rents are shown in box 7.4.

Regulatory accounting should be guided by a set of principles that make the gathered information a reflection of the financial reality of the regulated firm and useful for the regulator to perform his or her duties. For example, the information should assess bona fide and relevant costs, disentangle tasks performed by the operator and revenues that are subject to regulation from those which are not, allocate costs appropriately, assess the market value of investments, and so forth. Box 7.5 shows the general principles that should rule an effective regulatory accounting system.

To illustrate the importance of a sound regulatory accounting, tables 7.6, 7.7, and 7.8 show the impact of proper use and analysis of regulatory accounting for diverse sectors such as electricity distribution, gas, and water.

Box 7.4 *Common Questionable Actions That Need to Be Addressed through Regulatory Accounting*

A number of actions typically undertaken by operators affect their rate of return and have to be accounted for and carefully evaluated by the regulator—but often are not—because of their potential impact on tariff setting. The following are the most common:

- Excessive management fees—often equivalent to half of the firm net's profits
- Contracting subsidiaries or related companies to provide services or equipment at significantly higher prices than standard market prices
- Inflated investments proceeds
- Transfer of accumulated profits into the regulated capital base
- Transfer of capital in nonregulated areas of the firm into the regulated capital base of the firm
- Valuation of preprivatized assets at replacement costs
- Using, when convenient, past performance as justification for demands for future higher tariffs

---

The tables show components of the balance sheets of the regulated companies in those sectors in the United Kingdom, stating the average capital employed, the operating profit, and the resulting rate of return. The objective is to infer if indeed a tariff adjustment would be needed to secure the contracted rate of return.

The results from stated numbers from the regulated company show rates of return of capital around 9.7 percent, on average, for the distribution of electricity companies, but when the accounting is properly remodeled, the rates of return for capital climb to 22.5 percent, a significant difference that suggests no need for a tariff increase, because the rate of return sufficiently exceeds the desired and contracted rate of return. Similarly for the gas companies, the stated rate of return on average is around 6.4 percent, but when remodeled, it jumps to 14.8 percent. For the water companies the numbers are even more dramatic, because the rate of return as stated is about, on average, 0.9 percent, but when properly remodeled, it jumps to 18.3 percent.

These dramatic differences are generated by restating the CCA accounts of the regulated industries to reflect economic value principles, in this case by reflecting acquisition costs and the application of financial capital maintenance principles (see Carey and others 1994). The recalculated rates of

Box 7.5 *General Principles for Regulatory Accounting*

The regulatory accounting theory stipulates that the information used by the regulator should reflect with precision the reality of the firm. Consequently, regulatory accounting should establish principles that (a) ensure the accurateness and veracity of the information collected, and (b) provide a general guideline in those cases in which the norm and the regulator's criteria do not have enough precision to redefine the accounting principles.

More specifically, regulatory accounting should apply the following general accounting principles:

- *Causality.* Revenues, costs, assets, and financial obligations should be allocated according to each activity that generates them.
- *Objectivity.* The allocation should be based on objective principles and should not imply any undue benefit to any organization or individual.
- *Transparency.* The methodology of assignation should be clear. The accounts should be clearly distinguishable.
- *Coherence.* The allocation criteria should be constant from one year to another; however, in case of changes (for example, in the accounting method), the company should provide the necessary revisions and explanations for such modifications.
- *Materiality.* An accounting departure is considered material if its omission and misrepresentation has the potential to alter the financial position or the nature of the company's regulated and unregulated services.
- *Neutrality.* Internal transferences of costs and revenues should be transparent and in accordance with an applicable standard cost.
- *Sufficiency.* The information should comply with the requirements established according to the norm.
- *Disaggregation.* The costs imputed to services should be previously assigned to each particular activity that generates these services.

return differ from those stated in the accounts for two reasons. First, the value of the preprivatization assets has been reduced to acquisition cost and the depreciation charge associated with these assets is correspondently reduced. Subsequent additions are left at indexed replacement cost, because these assets are to be remunerated at the cost of capital. Assets in nonregulated businesses have not been written down (even if the market valued them below replacement cost), because the companies concerned have not thought that a write-down to below replacement cost was necessary. Second, accumulated profits should not be allowed to enter into the

Table 7.6 *Adjusted Results for Regional Electricity Distribution Companies (March 1991–March 1992)*

Distribution company	As stated			As remodeled		
	Average CCA capital employed (£ millions)	CCA operating profit (£ millions)	CCA rate of return (percent)	Average CCA capital employed (£ millions)	CCA operating profit (£ millions)	CCA rate of return (percent)
Eastern	1,316.2	120.4	9.1	718.4	155.3	21.6
EME	998.0	107.2	10.7	628.6	128.4	20.4
London	1,060.4	111.0	10.5	541.8	96.7	17.8
MANWEB	671.0	77.8	11.6	358.3	96.7	27.0
Midlands	1,021.7	94.7	9.3	542.0	121.6	22.4
Northern	617.9	59.1	9.6	313.9	80.8	25.7
NORWEB	890.7	81.4	9.1	468.6	95.1	20.3
SEEBOARD	702.0	49.9	7.1	244.0	89.2	36.6
Southern	1,035.7	121.3	11.7	660.5	143.1	21.7
South Wales	467.4	43.4	9.3	261.6	59.5	22.7
SWEB	743.2	60.5	8.1	346.6	84.1	24.3
Yorkshire	915.7	89.4	9.8	531.0	112.9	21.3
Average			9.7			22.5

Source: Carey and others (1994).

Table 7.7 *Adjusted Results for British Gas*

Period	As stated			As remodeled		
	Average CCA capital employed (£ millions)	CCA operating profit (£ millions)	CCA rate of return (percent)	Average CCA capital employed (£ millions)	CCA operating profit (£ millions)	CCA rate of return (percent)
March 1987	17,597	1,005	5.7	7,480	1,300	17.4
March 1988	17,318	1,053	6.1	7,774	1,321	17.0
March 1989	18,021	1,120	6.2	9,072	1,358	15.0
March 1990	19,795	1,095	5.5	11,042	1,292	11.7
March 1991	21,439	1,655	7.7	12,674	1,821	14.4
December 1991	22,550	1,673	7.4	13,410	1,830	13.6
Average			6.4			14.8

Source: Carey and others (1994).

Table 7.8 *Adjusted Results for Water Services Companies,*
March 1991–March 1992

Company	As stated			As remodeled		
	Average CCA capital employed (£ millions)	CCA operating profit (£ millions)	CCA rate of return (percent)	Average CCA capital employed (£ millions)	CCA operating profit (£ millions)	CCA rate of return (percent)
Anglian	10,531.3	164.9	1.6	907.5	192.1	21.2
Northumbria	3,252.9	27.5	0.8	89.0	39.0	43.8
North West	18,860.0	206.6	1.1	1,094.9	224.0	20.5
Severn Trent	19,847.7	168.9	0.9	1,053.3	232.2	22.0
Southern	9,528.8	43.6	0.5	469.1	68.6	14.6
South West	3,629.4	59.2	1.6	479.9	65.9	13.7
Thames	34,267.7	194.7	0.6	1,513.0	216.0	14.3
Welsh	7,396.2	102.3	1.4	429.4	126.7	29.5
Wessex	5,242.0	44.1	0.8	334.0	56.6	17.0
Yorkshire	11,875.8	97.1	0.8	958.8	117.2	12.2
Average			0.9			18.3

Source: Carey and others (1994).

capital base, because they were included in the firms' financial statements and disallowed by the regulator. Profits are liquid assets, already earning a return, and are risk free. Only when those profits are properly invested should they enter into the capital base. Third, the depreciation charges are evaluated on the basis of financial rather than operating capital maintenance: thus reductions in asset value that arise because of differences between general and asset specific inflation are charged to the profit-and-loss account. Also, variations in the depreciation charge that arise because of short-term fluctuations in the real value of assets or because of changes in methods of indexation were eliminated. Assets are indexed at the rate of general inflation, and a correction is made to account for the difference between specific and general inflation that arises because of technological change. These examples are just some of the ways that different interpretations of variables can affect the imputed rate of return significantly.

This example comes from the United Kingdom, where expertise in regulatory accounting is quite extensive. In developing countries, where those skills are less prevalent, the possibilities for misuse and manipulation are even greater, thus the need arises to clarify the rules of the game, to watch out for those practices, and to develop regulatory accounting expertise within the regulatory agency as soon as possible.

Addressing Termination of the Concession and Dispute Resolution

Any concession contract should address both how and under what conditions the concession can be terminated and how to handle dispute resolution. It should also demand a performance bond to ensure incentives for compliance and collection in the event of nonperformance. In particular the contract should contain the following:

- An initial performance bond for a concession contract. To provide enough high-power incentive, this bond should not be less than (a) 2 percent of the total value of the contract and (b) 20 percent of the estimated annual revenue of the concession in its first year.
- The circumstances under which the contract can be terminated. The compensation payable on termination should be defined in detail, referring, as appropriate, to the provisions of the federal law on concessions and any relevant state legislation if applicable.
- What happens at the end of the concession period. These provisions should include (a) the possibility of renewal of the concession, (b) the transitional arrangements if a new operator takes over the concession, and (c) the basis for calculating compensation for un-depreciated assets must be defined.
- Clauses that establish a basis for using arrangements for dispute resolution prior to recourse to the courts, such as the following:
  - Binding arbitration may not be legally or politically acceptable, but it is possible for the two parties to agree in the contract to the appointment of a panel of experts at the beginning of the concession to whom disputes may be referred by either party.
  - The panel of experts would normally be appointed by the federal sector agency and would include specialists in technical, economic, and legal aspects of the sector.
  - In disputes about technical issues, the parties could agree to refer the questions to a single adjudicator rather than the panel to obtain a rapid decision.
  - In the event of an appeal to the courts, the contract would state that the decision of the panel of experts should be implemented by the concessionaire on a temporary basis until a final court judgment is reached.

Arbitration Rules Stated in Concession Contract

Disputes among the operator, regulator, and government are standard and bound to arise under any contractual agreement. To reduce the regulatory risk induced by uncertainty on resolution of disputes, an arbitration mechanism that all parties perceived to be neutral and independent should be used. Thus the contract should contain various provisions for arbitration in the event of disputes between the concessionaire and either the regulator or the corresponding government, and should require that the rulings of an arbitration should be implemented on a provisional basis, with interim remedies in place even when they are appealed in the courts, because the appeal process can be significantly lengthy.

Institutional Structure of Regulatory Agencies

The quality of enforcement matters significantly in predicting sector performance, affecting renegotiation, and reducing regulatory risks. That quality of enforcement translates not only into having a regulatory agency in place, but also into having the right regulatory structure, organization, instruments, and appropriate financing, so the agency can effectively perform its assigned functions.

The essential functions of regulatory institutions are the following:

- Administering tariff adjustments and periodic reviews
- Establishing detailed quality and technical standards
- Monitoring compliance with contractual and legal regulatory requirements
- Imposing penalties for operators' noncompliance
- Facilitating the resolution of disputes between sector operators and between operators and consumers
- Providing advice and counsel to government on related matters and policy and licenses, and concession design
- Compiling information on operators' costs and performance and benchmarking operators' performance.

To perform the required functions effectively, the agency should be designed with the following features in place: board structure, term, qualifications, removal-from-office rules, salary rules, financing, safeguards on independence, safeguards on accountability, consultation structure, appeal structure, user complaint procedures, and institutional development and regulatory instruments. Each is outlined here.

Board Structure

The standard configuration for the decisionmaking body is one to five commissioners.

Term

Terms of about four to six years tend to be the usual. Terms should overlap the political election cycle and be longer than the term of office of the government. The term should not be renewable, except in unusual contexts, so the process and the regulatory decisions do not become politically contaminated because regulators might seek to ensure re-election. The terms of the different commissioners should be staggered to keep continuity.

Qualifications

Board members should have technical expertise. They should be professionals in public service or have academic experience related to regulated activities. They should be disqualified for conflict of interest. Consumers' representatives or operators' representatives should not be represented on the board.

Removal-from-Office Rules

Commissioners may be removed from office only for duly proven neglect, noncompliance, incompetence, conflict of interest, or immorality.

Salary Rules

The objective is to be able to attract outstanding professionals, thus salaries comparable to the private sector should be paid. To that extent the regulatory agency should be exempt from civil service salary rules.

Financing

The budget for the regulatory agency should come from levies from the regulated industry, a percentage of gross revenues from regulated companies. The usual percentage ranges from 0.5 to 2 percent, depending on the scale of operation. The operating budget should not be assigned as a part of the general government budget, as is done in many countries. Doing so allows for the possibility of government interference—cutting the budget— to influence regulatory decisions.

Safeguards on Independence

To avoid any form of capture by interested parties, independence requires arm's length relationships with regulated operators, consumer groups, and other private-interest groups and also an arm's length relationship with political authorities. The latter requires formal detachment of the agency from the corresponding ministry. Implementation of the items above would go a long way to secure that independence.

Safeguards on Accountability

To secure effectiveness and avoid autocratic and arbitrary behavior, independence must be complemented with strong accountability. Such accountability entails rigorous transparency requirements, open decisionmaking, and publication of decisions along with the reasons for those decisions. Regular public reporting should include information on appeals of regulators' decisions, performance scrutiny by public audit offices, budget scrutiny by the state legislature, and removal from office for misconduct or incapacity.

Consultation Structure

Although the boards should not include interested parties and stakeholders, institutionalizing public hearings and consultation processes is highly desirable. This institutionalization should occur periodically but particularly prior to major decisions, such as tariff adjustments and reviews, so all interested parties can have their say, present information, and influence decisions.

Appeal Structure

This component is essential for due process and accountability. Conflicts or disagreements between the regulator and the operator are bound to occur. An appeals process must be provided. Given the usual highly technical content of the issues, using special bodies as appeals forums, before going to the judicial system, is advisable.

User Complaint Procedures

Queries and complaints from users regarding components of the service are a part of normal operations. They should be handled and processed by the operator. When the users are not satisfied with the actions from the operator, the regulator can have jurisdiction to rule on the dispute. To be effective, this appeal function must be loaded with incentives. That is, the user filing an appeal is charged with a fee, reimbursable if the ruling is in its favor, and the operator is assigned a significant penalty if the ruling is in favor of the user. Various types of incentive-compatible penalties schemes can be implemented. For example, a certain number of cases ruled against the operator annually could be assessed no penalty, and an increasing marginal penalty per adverse case could be imposed beyond that number.

Institutional Development and Regulatory Instruments

The main objectives of a regulatory framework are (a) to induce the regulated firm to operate at lowest (efficient) possible costs and (b) to align prices (tariffs) closely with costs allowing the firm to earn only normal profits. Usually other subordinate objectives complement the main ones as well, such as to induce increased coverage and access, improve quality of service, and to address issues of universal service obligations. To secure those objectives effectively, the agency needs significant professional capacity and the appropriate information and regulatory instruments. The main issues are as follows:

- *Professional development:* To a large extent the success of a regulatory undertaking depends on the technical capacity of the regulators. Excellent laws and proper design of regulatory institutions, although essential, need to be complemented with highly qualified professionals to secure the expected benefits of regulation. To that extent, foreseeing not only the training of professionally selected regulators and technicians, but also the development of a stock of highly qualified professionals, is essential. High turnover is quite common and should be expected, because regulators migrate to the private sector or elsewhere, thus creating the need to ensure the existence of a steady stock of sector professionals. For that purpose the coordination of the federal government with universities and institutes to facilitate the provision of extensive programs in the economics of regulation is essential for the long-term sustainability of regulatory institutions and for their effectiveness

- *Technical support:* The agencies should have access to a direct or shared technical unit of support to undertake the in-depth technical studies required for effective tariff adjustments and reviews. That unit would be usually composed of sector economist, lawyers, and engineers.
- *Accounting and informational standards:* To improve effectiveness, the regulatory agencies should develop accounting and informational standards that facilitate the processing of information from operators and the evaluation of the concessionaire's performance.
- *Cost and financial models:* The regulators should develop cost and financial models of the operations of the regulated firm. Such instruments are essential for the process of tariff setting, and reviewing firms' adjustments demands evaluation of trigger variables.
- *Benchmarking exercises:* Regulatory agencies should have access to comparable indicators on performance from other water operator companies in- and outside the country, for the purpose of benchmarking. That information can be used quite effectively in the tariff adjustment and review exercise.

8

Conclusion

Since the late 1980s, an extraordinary flurry of reforms in the infrastructure sectors in Latin America and the Caribbean region has taken place. Traditional state-owned companies were restructured, unbundled, and privatized or concessioned to the private sector—over 1,000 of them. Concession contracts transferring the rights for the provision of infrastructure services to the private sector were drawn and signed, regulatory frameworks were put in place, and regulatory agencies were created. All that was driven by countries' understanding of the importance of infrastructure for sustained economic growth and for poverty alleviation, and by the need for significant amounts of needed investment and improvements in operative efficiency. That realization was the rational for bringing in the private sector. Given that most infrastructure sectors display aspects of natural monopoly— economies of scale—and that many of the investments in the sector tend to be of the sunk type, the strategy also called for the setting up of regulatory frameworks and agencies, recognizing the need both to address domestic concerns about monopolistic abuses by private (and mostly foreign) operators and to restrict government opportunistic behavior that would hamper foreign interest and investment in the sector.

After more than 15 years of accumulated experience of that reform program, an evaluation of the results was in order, and this book contributes toward that task. A number of studies, mostly country or sector based, have been undertaken for that purpose. In general they show that, overall, the program has produced significant benefits, particularly high-efficiency gains, improved quality of service, fair amounts of private investment, and increased coverage. Yet, the expectations were high and seldom fully met, and users have raised concerns, real or perceived, about the effectiveness of the model. Those concerns have grown over the years and have threatened the future of the reform program in a number of countries. Serious doubts have arisen about its efficacy, and acrimonious disputes over contract compliance, complaints about excessive tariffs, frequent bankruptcy claims by the concessionaires, reports of poor service delivery, and in particular, incidents of opportunistic renegotiation have come to the fore. The excessive proportion of renegotiated contracts and the quick renegotiations, here documented, strongly suggest opportunistic behavior and seriously flawed concession and regulatory design. This aspect of performance has been the motivation and the subject of this book. Early and frequent renegotiation affects sector performance; it also undermines the credibility of the process and the reputation of the country. I have shown that both governments and operators have abused the process to the detriment of future investment sector performance and overall welfare.

The lessons from this research are clear and ample. After evaluating the evidence, I conclude that the conceptual model behind the reform program was and remains sound. The problem has been in its faulty implementation. I have used renegotiation as an—albeit imperfect—proxy for performance and a symbol of the problems with the implementation of the model. I have identified the determinants of renegotiation and have provided policy and concession and regulatory design recommendations on how to improve them and to dissuade and reduce opportunistic renegotiation. Most of the opportunistic renegotiations could have been and should be avoided or dissuaded. Most of the mistakes made in the implementation process could have been avoided and should be avoided in future concessions by improved design and better attention to incentive structures. The key factors driving success in improving sector performance through private sector participation are an appropriate concession design and regulatory framework, and in most countries both have been riddled with mistakes and oversights. The best regulation cannot undo problems and mistakes made in the concession contract, and the best concession design will not be effective without proper regulatory oversight and enforcement. All the evidence indicates that those factors are basic and crucial. Proper design and built in, thorough contractual incentives ought to facilitate credibility on the stability of contractual terms and regulatory framework and induce or increase compliance by both signatory parties with the agreed-upon terms in the contract, something that has seldom happened. The high incidence of renegotiation bears witness to that fact. The main challenge of infrastructure concessions is writing time-consistent, enforceable contracts that cover all the contingencies that might arise with such technically complex activities and economic uncertainty and to signal credible commitment to a policy of not renegotiating opportunistic requests. Frequently, assumptions that seemed reasonable when planners developed the key economic parameters of a contract have proven highly inaccurate after the fact. Thus, allowing some room for renegotiation and regulatory adaptation may seem appropriate and socially desirable in the face of new problems, changed circumstances, and additional information and experience. Contractual incompleteness, however, could and has led to opportunistic renegotiation. In industrial countries, such renegotiation is not a big concern, though, because adherence to contracts can be enforced by high-quality institutions (Laffont and Tirole 1993). The absence of such institutional mechanisms in developing countries makes renegotiation a serious public policy issue that should be addressed.

I have documented and tested the fact that the high incidence of concession renegotiation can be attributed to weak regulatory governance, politics (political cycle and opportunism), flawed contract design, and external shocks. Setting up a separate and autonomous regulatory body appears to reduce renegotiations significantly. With a proper concession design and regulatory framework, contingencies occurring during the lifetime of the concession can then be dealt with through the normal revision process inside the regulatory framework, reducing the need for disruptive renegotiation. Having a regulatory body can also signal a commitment to enforcement and may signify experience in dealing with complex design issues and contracts, and having a regulatory agency be autonomous can signal to investors a welcome hands-off policy by the government. Using explicit long-term contracts, as was often the case for earlier concessions in Latin America and the Caribbean, as a substitute for separate regulatory institutions is likely to be problematic. Without an independent mediating regulator, any adaptations must be renegotiated with the government, and this need increases the risk of harmful political interference, as has often been the case. If, however, concessions are lodged within a separate regulatory framework that defines the basis and criteria for contract revision, socially desirable, dynamic adaptations would be feasible and less likely to place significant strain on concessions facing uncertain economic conditions. This advantage applies, in particular, to concession contracts for roads and railroads, for example, because demand for such services is subject to large fluctuations, and cost estimates are frequently not very reliable.

Improved allocation of risk in the concession contract and regulatory framework (in concordance with the general economic principles of risk allocation to reduce the cost of capital and improved informational requirements) ought to be given greater attention because they affect investment levels and sector performance. An example is the choice of the regulatory regime. The evidence shows that price caps are more conducive to renegotiation, possibly because, relative to cost-plus rules, price caps shift more of the risk from consumers to the operating entities. This finding is especially important for policy in Latin America, where price caps regulate most concessions.

Faulty concession contract design has been another key driver of renegotiations and conflict by opening doors and providing opportunities for revisiting the contract and reducing incentives for compliance. There, the issues are multiple, ranging from improper award criteria, use of investment obligations, ambiguous regulatory accounting, valuation and components of the asset base, and ambiguous tariff adjustment procedures to low-value performance bonds, sweeping and misused financial equilibrium clauses, lack of clarity in procedures for dispute resolution, and so on, but all are relatively easy to fix. Fixing those problems for future concessions would also go a long way toward reducing renegotiation and improving sector performance.

To complement proper concession design, regulation, as the driver of postconcession governance, is critical to secure the benefits of an appropriate concession design and to serve as a dissuader and a filter for opportunistic renegotiations. I have already discussed the impact of the existence of the regulatory agency, but effective regulation obviously goes beyond the mere creation of a regulatory agency. The two main objectives of regulation are to induce firms to produce the service at the lowest possible costs—securing efficiency gains—and to align prices with those costs so that only normal profits are realized—passing those efficiency gains to the users. As we have seen, the latter has been an issue in Latin American and Caribbean countries and in essence a failure of regulation. A third complementary objective is to increase quality of service. Securing those objectives alone would facilitate increases in coverage, a key objective of the process of reform, because lower prices will increase demand for the service. The challenge is considerable, not only because the establishment and operation of an effective regulatory system is a complex undertaking and requires a learning process, but also because of the lack of a regulatory tradition and track record, the scarcity of expertise, and weak formal and informal norms protecting private rights—all so prevalent in developing countries. Moreover, the difficulty of establishing an effective regulatory regime is exacerbated by conflicting objectives (such as ensuring sector competition, high revenues from concession and privatization for fiscal reasons, ambitious investment demands, rapid expansion of basic services, and distributional factors in the pricing of the services) and the reluctance of most governments to relinquish control of the sector. Governments tempted to use regulation to advance short-term political goals, which have inappropriate regard for efficiency or implications for investors and information asymmetries in costs and performance that favor the operators, make the regulatory system vulnerable to capture, thus diminishing credibility and overall welfare. Information and commitment problems can undermine the efforts of even the most well-intentioned regulators.

Consequently, the development of the required and appropriate regulatory institutions, not surprisingly, has been slower than desired and has generated criticism, as illustrated here. Although the regulatory initiatives and activities have been many and varied, the results have been mixed, although improving. Although much work remains to be done in this area, both procedurally and substantively, the slow but steady achievements on the regulatory front in most developing countries is encouraging, particularly given the complexities just described. Many developing countries have enacted sectoral and regulatory framework laws, deregulated operations that should not have been regulated, established regulatory agencies, and so on, with a mixed degree of success. But indeed one should understand that this effort is a learning process, and that countries that are successful today took many years to secure a reliable and effective regulatory regime and associated enforcement. Most reassuring is that the awareness of the need to establish, and benefits of establishing, an effective regulatory regime appears to be growing, as is the commitment to the process.

Although direct regulation of aspects of the infrastructure sector continues to be necessary, technological innovations are making feasible the use of competition in many segments of utilities. The general principle is to regulate those segments of the market that display natural monopoly characteristics to curtail abuses of monopoly power, to protect consumers, given the lack of competitive alternatives of service, and to ensure access (fair price and quality of service) by would-be competitors to essential facilities that are often controlled by incumbent companies. At the same time, recognizing that technology and new entrants are eroding market power, governments should help this process along by fostering greater competition, passing antitrust legislation, providing regulatory credibility, and implementing large-scale deregulation to facilitate entry by potential market players exploiting the technological opportunities. I have noted that the presence of competition—potential or real—is a key factor in dissuading renegotiation, because that option provides the government with leverage to turn down opportunistic request. That aspect in part has contributed to the lower levels of renegotiations in the telecommunications and energy sectors. Thus efforts to facilitate competition ought to be part of the sector strategy to secure long-term sector efficiency (see among others Beato and Laffont 2002). Yet to complement that trend, countries must develop and enforce a competition policy framework to account and dissuade potential anticompetitive practices, not unusual in this context. The telecommunications sector provides an example in those countries where it has been open to competition and deregulated a number of segments, such as in Argentina, Brazil, Chile, El Salvador, Mexico, and Peru. The trend toward liberalization and increased competition, driven by technological innovation, is unquestionable, yet regulatory needs remain, particularly in the network component of the sectors.

The lessons from the theory and particularly from 15 years of experience in concessions and regulation in the Latin American and Caribbean region ought to prove most useful for countries in the midst of a reform program, either in fine-tuning or in furthering the program, or for countries just beginning infrastructure reform. Understanding that institutions and country endowments matter and that their capacity and levels ought to be taken into consideration, the requirements for a successful program of infrastructure reform based on private sector participation are as follows:

- Competitive concession award process
- Proper concession design
- Proper regulatory framework
- Proper sector restructuring
- Regulatory credibility
- Clear rules for and limits to government and regulator discretion
- Respect for and enforcement of the sanctity of the bid at the time of the auction
- Minimal opportunities for frivolous and opportunistic renegotiations
- Dissuasion through financial incentives of opportunistic renegotiations and development of a credible commitment to the nonrenegotiation of opportunistic petitions
- Costly unilateral changes of the agreed-upon contractual terms of the concession
- An incentive-based regulatory framework
- Appropriate regulatory and antitrust legislation

- Autonomous regulatory institutions, well-trained and well-compensated professionals, and effective enforcement
- An appropriate set of regulatory instruments, such as a regulatory accounting system, cost and financial models, and benchmarking referential data
- Competition in the provision of services in as much as it is feasible.

Complying with all those elements would go a long way toward creating an appropriate, credible, and predictable investment climate and restoring confidence of both private investors and dissatisfied users. Both are key for securing the most needed investments in the infrastructure sector and popular support for the reform program. Finally for all pieces to fit together, all administrative procedures, processes, rules, and decisions that are part of the implementation of concession contracts and the regulatory framework ought to be as transparent as possible. Appropriate enforcement should be forthcoming and in compliance with the mandate. Carefully designed concession contracts and regulatory policies and appropriate selection of regulatory instruments and regimes, when transparent and properly enforced, can increase a country's limited powers of commitment and the effectiveness of regulation. This confidence will promote private investors' confidence about the stability of the agreed-upon contractual terms and the regulatory framework and will limit the opportunities for regulatory capture from government, industry, or consumers. Needed investment, efficient provision, and increased competitiveness of productive users will follow. Formal and binding rules need to be specified precisely if they are to provide a credible anchor for concession contracts and the regulatory system. The mechanisms for rulemaking (law or legally binding contracts) need to be reasonably resilient to pressures for change. Institutions are needed to enforce both the specific restraints and the restraints on system changes and to provide well-defined and credible conflict resolution mechanisms. The overall benefits should be well understood, and they can be significant. Aside from increased efficiency and economic growth, the accompanying expansion of coverage has very positive effects on productivity opportunities and on poverty alleviation—the quality of life of individuals who have lower incomes and who previously were excluded from service or were offered very poor quality service. Consequently, the overall impact on welfare and income distribution can be considerable.

Appendix 1

Data Description

Data from around 1,000 concessions awarded from the mid-1980s to 2000 in the Latin American and Caribbean region were collected. The choice of that region was based on its being the pioneer in awarding concessions; by end of the century, the region already had a track record. These concession contracts signed between the governments and private enterprises encompass 17 countries in the Latin American and Caribbean region.

The dataset collected incorporates both modes of private sector participation: privatizations and concessions contracts. Practically all of the straight sale privatization transactions were in the telecommunications sector, although a few were in electricity generation. Practically all of the transactions in telecommunications were straight privatizations. Specifically, the cases of complete transfer of ownership (271 concessions) tended to be concentrated in the telecommunications subsector and were primarily auctions for the sale of state-owned company or auctions of bandwidth frequencies for an *indefinite period of time* with periodic predetermined license fee payment requirement, a very particular service and quite different from a standard concession.

For the econometric analysis to impute the determinants of renegotiations, only the data on concessions were used. The telecommunications data have been excluded from the analysis. The main reasons are, first, because concessions and privatizations are two different instruments and the large number of spectrum-related transactions can contaminate the results and, second, because my focus is essentially on concessions. In the case of full privatization, first, the issue of lack of ownership rights of the government and, second, the issue of not being duration-bound could be expected to alter the incentives and thereby the actions of agents and the government position. Because privatization is not time-bound and the government does not own the assets, privatization might strengthen the leverage of the government—not to mention the higher degree of competitiveness of the sector—and weaken the likelihood of renegotiation between the government and the concessionaire or operator in the future. For all these reasons, the telecommunications sector has been left out of the empirical analysis. Yet one sectoral element is worth noticing. The incidence of renegotiation in both the telecommunications sector and in the electricity sector is quite low, particularly when compared to that of the transportation and water sectors. A plausible explanation is the correlation with the degree of competitiveness within sectors. The less competitive sectors are water and sanitation and transportation, but electricity, and especially telecommunications, are much more competitive. In more competitive regimes, the government could have a higher leverage and a more credible commitment, if it were to choose so, not to renegotiate, because it could argue that if the agreed-upon contractual terms are now not desirable for the operator, it could leave the concession, and an existing operator (or maybe a potential one) could take it over or cover the slack relatively easily.

The broad orientation of the independent variables collected can be categorized into seven broad types.

1. General data	Includes macroinformation of the country, such as the country code, the GDP per capita, exchange rate (to account for significant devaluations), and corruption indexes.
2. Project data	Includes variables constructed that provide details of the concession as contracted upon and subsequently stated in the contract.
3. Award of concession	Includes type of process—competitive versus noncompetitive—and variables constructed that detail the process and criteria of selection of the contract award winner.
4. Regulation	Includes variables that detail the regulatory regime and framework within which the operation and performance of the concession is evaluated. Additional variables constructed incorporate the structure, composition, autonomy, and functioning of the regulatory agencies.

5. Concession details   Includes variables that are constructed to offer additional details pertaining to the operation of the contract, such as frequency of tariff reviews and tariff adjustment, government guarantees, some contractual obligations of the concessionaire, and stipulations of contract renewals.

6. Concession renegotiation   Includes variables that denote the implications of a contract failure, in terms of the causes and also the outcome.

7. Risk   Devises variables that portray the risk bearing of the concession.

I present below a set of summary statistics from the dataset, complementing those shown in chapter 6 (tables A1.1 through A1.8).

Table A1.1 *Concessions in Dataset by Year of Origin, 1982–2000*

Year of the concession	Frequency	As a percentage	Cumulative frequency
1982	1	0.11	0.11
1985	2	0.22	0.33
1987	1	0.11	0.45
1988	4	0.45	0.89
1989	11	1.23	2.12
1990	33	3.68	5.80
1991	21	2.34	8.15
1992	36	4.02	12.17
1993	51	5.69	17.86
1994	63	7.03	24.89
1995	75	8.37	33.26
1996	74	8.26	41.52
1997	206	22.99	64.51
1998	188	20.98	85.49
1999	120	13.39	98.88
2000	10	1.12	100.00
Total	896	100.00	

Note: Data may not sum to totals because of rounding.

Table A1.2 Concession Awarded by Year and Country, 1982–2000

Year	Argentina	Bolivia	Brazil	Chile	Colombia	Costa Rica	Ecuador	Guatemala	Jamaica	Mexico	Panama	Peru	Trinidad and Tobago	Uruguay	Venezuela	Total
1982	0	0	0	0	0	0	0	0	0	0	0	1	0	0	0	1
1985	0	0	0	0	0	2	0	0	0	0	0	0	0	0	0	2
1987	0	0	0	0	0	0	0	0	0	1	0	0	0	0	0	1
1988	0	0	0	0	0	1	0	0	2	1	0	0	0	0	0	4
1989	2	0	0	0	0	0	0	0	0	9	0	0	0	0	0	11
1990	16	0	0	0	0	3	0	0	0	14	0	0	0	0	0	33
1991	2	0	0	0	0	1	0	0	0	16	0	0	0	0	2	21
1992	16	0	0	1	1	5	0	0	0	12	0	0	0	0	1	36
1993	14	0	0	0	5	4	0	0	0	24	1	3	0	0	0	51
1994	11	0	3	2	12	7	0	0	0	18	0	8	1	1	0	63
1995	14	6	13	4	4	3	0	0	0	15	0	15	1	0	0	75
1996	0	9	23	5	8	3	0	0	0	11	1	15	0	0	1	76
1997	6	4	56	78	10	0	0	0	0	37	3	12	0	0	0	206
1998	6	2	87	9	6	2	0	3	0	58	0	14	0	10	0	197
1999	12	5	8	7	4	0	2	0	0	42	0	39	0	10	0	129
2000	0	0	0	4	1	0	0	0	0	4	0	0	0	1	0	10
Total	99	26	190	110	51	31	2	3	2	262	5	107	2	22	4	916

Table A1.3 *Number of Bidders by Sector, Not Including Bilateral Negotiation—Direct Adjudication*

Number of bidders	Communications	Energy	Transportation	Water
0	0	1	0	2
1	0	3	39	10
2	0	5	66	54
3	2	6	33	29
4	0	9	16	6
5	3	3	8	0
6	8	5	10	2
7	0	2	7	0
8	0	2	0	0
9	0	0	2	0
11	0	0	1	0
12	10	3	0	0
13	0	3	0	0
14	7	0	0	0
17	13	0	0	0
22	18	0	0	0
23	4	0	0	0

Table A1.4 *Correlation of Incidence of Renegotiation and Degree of Competitiveness in the Sector*

Low incidence— more competitive sectors	High incidence— less competitive sectors
Telecommunications and energy	Transportation and water and sewage

Table A1.5 *Incidence of Concession Renegotiation, Selected Countries, 1986–2000*

Year	Argen-tina	Bolivia	Brazil	Chile	Colombia	Costa Rica	Mexico	Total
1986	0	0	0	0	0	0	0	0
1987	0	0	0	0	0	0	1	1
1988	0	0	0	0	0	0	1	1
1989	1	0	0	0	0	0	9	10
1990	14	0	0	0	0	0	14	28
1991	2	0	0	0	0	0	13	15
1992	1	0	0	0	1	0	4	6
1993	8	0	0	0	2	0	15	25
1994	4	0	3	0	10	0	15	32
1995	6	0	12	2	3	1	8	32
1996	0	0	18	2	6	0	3	29
1997	3	0	13	1	4	0	4	25
1998	3	0	26	0	1	0	3	33
1999	0	1	0	3	1	0	0	5
2000	3	2	0	2	0	0	0	7

Table A1.6 Selected Summary Statistics for the Transportation and Water Sectors

Summary statistics	Total transportation and water				Transportation				Water			
	Yes	Percent	No	Percent	Yes	Percent	No	Percent	Yes	Percent	No	Percent
Renegotiations initiated by firms	53	17.3	254	82.7	49	22.5	169	77.5	4	4.5	85	95.5
Renegotiations initiated by government	94	30.6	213	69.4	35	16.1	183	83.9	59	66.3	30	33.7
Renegotiation initiated by both	15	4.9	292	95.1	15	6.9	203	93.1	0	0.0	89	100.0
Existence of regulatory body	180	58.6	127	41.4	168	77.1	50	22.9	12	13.5	77	86.5
Bidding process	272	88.6	35	11.4	185	84.9	33	15.1	87	97.8	2	2.2
Investment requirements	235	76.5	72	23.5	198	90.8	20	9.2	37	41.6	52	58.4
Private financing only	160	52.1	147	47.9	139	63.8	79	36.2	21	23.6	68	76.4
Price-cap regulation	283	92.2	24	7.8	199	91.3	19	8.7	84	94.4	5	5.6
Rate-of-return regulation	23	7.5	284	92.5	19	8.7	199	91.3	4	4.5	85	95.5
Arbitration process	179	58.3	128	41.7	172	78.9	46	21.1	7	7.9	82	92.1
Minimum income guarantee	63	20.5	244	79.5	62	28.4	156	71.6	1	1.1	88	98.9

Table A1.7 *Transportation Sector Incidence of Renegotiated Concession Contracts According to Characteristics*

Feature	Incidence of renegotiation (percent)
Award criteria	
Minimum tariff	60
High Price	32.5
Regulation criteria	
Regulation by means (investments)	76
Regulation by objectives (performance indicators)	19
Regulatory framework	
Price cap	59.13
Rate of return	35.10
Existence of regulatory body	
Regulatory body in existence	31.24
Regulatory body not in existence	62.50
Impact of the legal framework	
When regulatory framework imbedded in law	55.56
When regulatory framework imbedded in contract	70.73

Table A1.8 *Water Sector Incidence of Renegotiated Concession Contracts According to Characteristics*

Feature	Incidence of renegotiation (percent)
Award criteria	
Lowest tariff	81.90
High price	66.6
Regulation criteria	
Regulation by means (investments)	85
Regulation by objectives (performance indicators)	25
Regulatory framework	
Price cap	88.79
Rate of return	14.29
Existence of regulatory body	
Regulatory body in existence	40.91
Regulatory body not in existence	87.50
Impact of the legal framework	
When regulatory framework imbedded in law	55.56
When regulatory framework imbedded in decree	83.33
When regulatory framework imbedded in contract	70

Appendix 2

Choice and Definition of Independent Variables

The principle is to estimate the impact of various explanatory variables on the probability of renegotiation, that is, the determinants of renegotiation. The choice of the independent—explanatory—variables is guided by the theory of contracts and institutions. The hypotheses, driven by the theory, to be tested are the impact on the probability of renegotiation of external shocks, quality of enforcement, financial structure of project, extent of competitiveness, extent of affiliation, tariff adequacy and lock-in components, legal grounding of regulation, ease of overseeing contractual obligations, allocation of risk, and reputation and learning. These factors and the variables or proxies used to evaluate their impact are described in this appendix.

Definition of Terms

The estimation is a probit analysis, and to ensure consistency, various models are tested to impute the significance and marginal impact of those key variables in the probability of renegotiation. This section presents the choice and definition of the explanatory variables and the econometrics estimates of the probit model. In all models the dependent variable is the probability of renegotiation. The factors listed in this section, as determinants of renegotiation, are incorporated in the equation.

External Shocks

A GDP variable and an exchange rate variable are used to account for the impact of external shocks that might affect the financial viability of concessions and trigger demands for renegotiation. An example of the potential effect of a macroeconomic shock on renegotiation incidence is the dissolution of Argentina's Convertibility Law in 2002, which led to renegotiations of practically all concessions of infrastructure services. That event is not covered in this book's data and analysis, which end in late 2001.

The Strength of the Legal Foundation of Regulation

The principle here is to test the strength of the legal foundations of regulation. The regulatory framework can be embodied into a law, decree, contract, or license. Each one provides different signals about the degrees of stability of the framework, and how difficult it would be to change it. That stability, in principle, could affect the likelihood of renegotiation. One would expect that the stronger the legal grounding, the less likely the renegotiation.

The Quality of Enforcement

Two variables are used to capture this factor. One is the existence of a regulatory agency, and the second is its autonomy. In its absence or if it is not autonomous, the interpretation is a weaker quality of enforcement and an increased probability of renegotiation.

Allocation of Risks

The risk allocation is captured here under the type of regulation. That is, a price-cap regulatory regime allocates risk to the operator, and a rate-of-return regulation transfers that risk to the government. The higher the risk bearing of the operator, the more likely the renegotiation.

Award Process

This variable refers to the type of process used to assign the concession as competitive or noncompetitive—direct adjudication or bilateral negotiations. The hypothesis here is that the competitive process should increase the likelihood of renegotiation.

Award Criteria

A variety of criteria have been used to assign concessions competitively. The most common are the following.

- *Highest price or canon*—in which "canon" denotes either a single payment at the award of the concession or periodic payments (for example, an annuity) so that the award criteria would have been the present discounted value of the future expected flows of income from the concessionaire to the government. Periodic payments are rarely used.
- *Lowest tariff*—in which the selection criterion is the lowest tariff the concessionaire commits at the bidding.
- *Lowest government subsidy*—in which the concession is awarded to the bidder who seeks the minimal subsidy support from the government to fulfill its service obligations.
- *Best investment/business plan*—in which the award criterion is a complex of business plans that includes service parameters and investment commitments.
- *Shortest duration of concession*—in which the award of the concession is made to the bidder seeking the shortest duration of exclusive operating rights before transfer of the asset and its operations to the government.
- *Multiple criteria*—in which a combination of factors is used, including some of the above. Factors might or might not be linked through a scoring function to determine the relative weights used on those various factors to determine the winner. The reasons the award criteria might matter in the incidence of renegotiation are various. First, it induces different levels of lock-in costs and thus implicit commitment or costs of abandoning the concession. For example, a tariff criterion does not involve any transfer of funds, but a transfer fee or canon does. Second, some variables such as tariffs are reviewed and negotiated on a fairly continuous basis, but transfer fees and canons are not and are thus more likely to be changed and renegotiated. And third, this variable can be thought of as a proxy for tariff adequacy. Competitive bidding via lowest tariff is likely to lead to inadequacy of tariffs and more likely renegotiation.

The Impact of Affiliation

To test for the opportunity and ability to renegotiate, the nationality of the operator is used as a proxy. The hypothesis is that domestic operators might have stronger ties to the government, and those ties might facilitate renegotiation.

The General Environment

A country corruption index is used to impute the impact of the country's level of corruption on the incidence of renegotiation. The hypothesis is that the higher the corruption level, the more likely renegotiation.

Reputation Effect

To test for the reputation effect and learning curve, a variable measuring the number of concessions previously granted in the country is used. This variable might have two effects working in opposite directions. The learning curve component might lead to an eventual decline in renegotiations as the country learns to design better concessions. A country that has conceded on renegotiations, however, might open the door for increased demands for renegotiations, because current or future operators begin to realize that renegotiations may be likely.

Project Finance and Government Guarantees

Because some of the theory models indicate a possible impact on renegotiation on the financial structure of the project, two variables are used to test for that possibility: one to measure the existence of any form of government guarantees and the other to measure any form of government finance in the concession, other than guarantees.

Investment Requirements

The theory points out the possible impact of the extent of the sunk costs and investments on the probability of renegotiation. It is also a measure of ease of oversight of contract. Measuring realized investments and their value is always problematic and leads into conflicts. A proxy for that measure used here is the often-required investment obligation to the operator.

Political Economy

The empirical evidence shows that the behavior of governments is influenced by the politics of elections, and that new administrations, particularly when they are from a different party than the previous administration, tend to dishonor decisions made by the previous administration. An administration change has been often the cause for government-led renegotiations. To account for that factor, we used a dummy variable that indicates whether the year was an election year.

Detailed Description of the Variables

The complete coding of the variables in the dataset are the following.

The Dependent Variable: dreneg

The dependent variable is a binary variable such that *dreneg*
    = 1 if concession was renegotiated
    = 0 if concession was not renegotiated.

The Independent/Explanatory Variables

gdp	To account for possible impact of economic cycle on incidence of renegotiation, the rate of growth of GDP was used and complemented with exchange rate fluctuations to account for the impact of significant devaluations, given the debt exposure in foreign currency of operators and revenues in local currency.
dcp_bid	To account for the impact of the type of process used to award the concession, a variable, *dcp_bid*, was used to differentiate between concessions awarded competitively and those awarded by direct adjudication or bilateral negotiations. This dummy variable has the following values
	= 1 if the contract process was a bid
	= 0 if the contract process was anything other than a bid (such as direct adjudication/request/petition).
daward	On some concessions only one selection criterion was used to determine the award, whereas in others, a combination of a

few of these factors was used. For the strategic incentives, from the bidders' standpoint, those various criteria can be bundled into two: (a) those that relate to a transfer fee; and (b) the rest—lowest tariffs, lowest duration, investment plan, and so on. This dummy variable is created generated from the information above such that

1 = Award criteria of highest price, highest canon, or lowest subsidy (in short, based purely on monetary transfer considerations)

0 = All other possible award criteria (in which minimum tariffs criteria are the most frequent).

dreg This variable is a list of the types of regulatory framework in effect on the concession. The set includes law, decree, contract, or license. Because the regulatory institutions could be in effect in isolation or in combination with each other, the following dummies created for each of the three institutions allow calculation of the marginal impacts of each of them. The corresponding dummy variables are law, decree, and contract where

1 = Yes,

0 = No

for each of the three dummy variables.

rbexist This dummy variable lists the presence of an appropriate regulatory body at the time of the award of the concession. Here the regulatory body is defined as an agency other than the government, which in any case could be expected to possess some form of regulatory power.

rbmin This variable is a dummy to capture whether the regulatory body is constituted as a part of a government ministry or an autonomous agency detached from any ministry. The variable is designed as a proxy for the autonomy of the regulatory body.

dnatcon This variable is the dummy for *rbmin* such that

1 = Local or both local and foreign

0 = Foreign only.

govguar This variable specifies the existence of government guarantees offered to the concessionaires to aid their operation.

dtarreg This variable specifies the type of tariff regulation imposed by the regulatory body on the concessionaire. The major categories are the following:

- Revenue cap—which restricts the maximum level of revenue earnings permissible.
- Price cap—which includes price caps with quality indexes and flat, fixed, and basic tariffs, all of which stipulate the maximum charges that the service providers can impose on the service users.
- Rate-of-return cap—which allows for the earnings of a specified rate of return on investment and might include some restrictions on the type of costs allowed to pass through. This variable is a dummy to capture the different forms of tariff regulations. The combination used was

    dtarreg = 1 if price cap or revenue cap was the type of tariff regulation

    dtarreg = 0 if rate of return was the type of regulation. This variable is supposed to capture the impact of risk allocation. A rate-of-return framework transfers the risk of changes on some input costs and demand to the government, whereas under the other regime the risk is borne by the operator.

invest   This variable refers to any investment commitments required of the concessionaire as stipulated in the contract.

dprojfin   This variable is the dummy for the source of financial capital for the concession such that

    1 = When the project is funded entirely through private funds (without any financial investment of the state, whether local or national)

    0 = When both state and private investments account for the project funding.

ncon   This variable, which is the number of concessions signed within the same subsector in the same country prior to the particular contract, is intended to capture any systematic effects of learning from prior experience within the country from having negotiated previous concessions as well as the reputation and track record upon which the potential operators can build their beliefs.

elect1   This variable is a dummy to indicate if the year was an election year. This variable is supposed to capture the behavior of a new administration in honoring the contract signed by a previous administration.

exchra1   This variable measures the annual evolution of the real exchange rate—calculated as a rate of year t minus rate of year $t-1$ over the rate of year t. It is supposed to pick the impact of devaluations. This element is important, because in most concessions, revenues are collected in domestic currency, but equity and debt tend to be in foreign currency. I introduced a lag, because the government intervention usually happens shortly after the election, and not immediately.

texp   This variable attempts to measure the impact of country experience in granting concessions and to capture any systematic effects of learning from prior experience within the country from having negotiated previous concessions. It measures the number of concessions signed in the country in the years prior to the signing of that particular concession contract.

Main Variables Used as Independent Variables to Estimate Their Impact on the Probability of Renegotiation

In summary, for the econometric probit analysis, I have selected the following set of explanatory variables.

gdp   The rate of growth of the country's GDP.

exchra1   Exchange rate variable lagged by one year (Year t rate- year $(t-1)$/year t rate).

daward   Dummy for award criterion such that
        1 = High price, high canon, or low subsidy
        0 = Rest.

multcrit   Dummy for use of multicriteria to award concession
        1 = Multicriteria used
        0 = Single criterion used.

condur   The length of the concession, in number of years.

invest   The existence of investment commitments required of the concessionaire as in the contract, normalized in real 1996 U.S. dollars.

dreg   Dummy for regulatory environment such that
        1 = Law or decree or both
        0 = Other than either law or decree.

dgovguar	Dummy for government guarantees such that
	1 = Any form of government guarantee
	0 = No government guarantee.
rbexist1	Dummy for regulatory body to exist at the time of signing
	the contract such that
	1 = Regulatory body did exist
	0 = Regulatory body did not exist.
rbmin	Dummy for whether the regulatory body is a part of the
	ministry or not such that
	1 = Yes
	0 = No.
dtarreg2	Dummy for type of tariff regulation such that
	1 = Price cap
	0 = Rate of return.
dnatcon	Dummy for nationality of the concessionaire such that
	1 = Local or both
	0 = Foreign only.
dprojfin	Dummy for project finance such that
	1 = Entire private funds and no government funding
	0 = Private loans plus state funding.
ncon	Number of concessions signed in the same subsector in
	that country prior to the present concession.
dcp-bid	Dummy variable for type of award process such that
	1 = Competitive process
	0 = Noncompetitive process—direct adjudication or bi-
	lateral negotiations.
elect1	Dummy variable indicating whether an election was held
	in any given year, lagged by one year.
	1 = This was an election year in the country.
	0 = This was not an election year in the country.
corrupt	Country index of corruption (Kaufmann, Kraay, and Zoido-
	Lobaton 1999a).

Model Specifications

The independent variables to be tested for their significance and impact on the probability of renegotiation are here listed and described above: *gdp, daward, multcrit, condur, invest, dreg, dgovguar, rbexist1, rbmin, dtarreg2, dnatcon, dprojfin, ncon, elect1,* and *exchra1.* Four different model specifications were run described as M1, M2, M3, and M4. The models are chosen to account for the variables that the theory indicates are likely determinants of renegotiation. The variations among the models are small and reflect dropping variables from M1 that are not significant, or in one case to increase the sample size. Increasing the sample size was the reason for dropping project finance, because I did not have that information for a number of data points. The empty cells in the tables in appendix 3 indicate the variables dropped in M2, M3, and M4. Available variables that were not significant in the preliminary testing were not included in the models.

MODEL M1. The following variables were used to determine *dreneg:* GDP, award criteria, multicriteria, duration of concession, investment requirements, legal basis of regulation, existence of government guarantees, existence of regulatory agency, autonomy of regulatory agency, type of regulation, nationality of concession winner, structure of project finance, number of prior concessions granted in same subsector.

MODEL M2. The following variables were used to determine *dreneg:* GDP, award criteria, multicriteria, duration of concession, investment requirements, legal basis of regulation, existence of government guarantees, existence of regulatory agency, autonomy of regulatory agency, type of regulation, nationality of concession winner, number of prior concessions granted in same subsector.

MODEL M3. The following variables were used to determine *dreneg:* GDP, award criteria, multicriteria, duration of concession, investment requirements, legal basis of regulation, existence of regulatory agency, autonomy of regulatory agency, type of regulation, nationality of concession winner, structure of project finance, number of prior concessions granted in same subsector.

MODEL M4. The following variables were used to determine *dreneg:* GDP, award criteria, multicriteria, duration of concession, investment requirements, legal basis of regulation, existence of regulatory agency, autonomy of regulatory agency, type of regulation, nationality of concession winner, number of prior concessions granted in same subsector.

Appendix 3

Econometric Analysis: Results of the Probit Estimations

Summary Results

We explore various specifications and find a consistent set of significance in most of those key variables. The number of observations used in the estimation analysis is less than the total number of observations of concessions, the reason being that the data for some of the variables used were missing from the concession dataset. Yet, around 400 observations were used in the estimates. The four variations of the model and the estimated results—the marginal probabilities of renegotiation associated with the independent variables—are described below. The complete estimates are also presented in tables A1.1, A1.2, and A1.3.

A weakness of the econometric estimates is that, one could argue, contract clauses are endogenous. That issue is addressed in Guasch, Laffont, and Straub (2003). The endogenous nature of contracts' clauses has two dimensions.

First is an ex ante self-selection problem, because the contracting parties would select specific clauses, type of regulation, and financing according to their (sometimes unobservable) characteristics or to the characteristics of the project. For example, the inclusion of specific arbitration rules could be induced by the government's anticipation of potential renegotiations and of the firm's perceived renegotiation skills. Conversely, minimum income guarantee would be included as a means to make risky concessions attractive to private agents. A similar problem applies to the type of tariff regulation chosen. A self-selection effect would suggest that more efficient

Table A3.1 *Significance of Independent Variables on Probability of Renegotiation*

dreneg	M1 coefficient	M2 coefficient	M3 coefficient	M4 coefficient
gdp	.0000423	.0001708	.0000278	.0001705[c]
	(.0000837)	(.0000789)	(.0000803)	(.0000777)
daward[a]	−.9830498[b]	−1.585373[b]	1.108564[b]	−1.588311[b]
	(.3352856)	(.2688994)	(.2853372)	(.2471818)
compet[a]	.567126[b]			
	(.2082842)			
multcrit	.0252056	−.1149253	.0753693	−.1134499
	(.3023747)	(.2715943)	(.2929118)	(.269005)
condur	−.0392298[b]	−.0435871[b]	−.038092[b]	−.0435773[b]
	(.0066922)	(.0061395)	(.0064622)	(.006021)
Invest	.0010844[b]	.0006101[c]	.0011189[b]	.0006117[c]
	(.000333)	(.0002696)	(.0003331)	(.0002612)
dreg[a]	.6310063[c]	.2711393	.6020085[c]	.2716787
	(.2836421)	(.2487905)	(.2788054)	(.2483975)
dgovguar[a]	.2220923	.0048946		
	(.3168987)	(.2209425)		
rbexist1[a]	−1.423997[b]	−1.322838[b]	1.460583[b]	−1.322802[b]
	(.3936929)	(.3671021)	(.3921621)	(.3670613)
rbmin[a]	1.316816[b]	1.3559[b]	1.336007[b]	1.355659[b]
	(.3781053)	(.3321795)	(.3793908)	(.3312332)
dtarreg2[a]	.6578784[c]	.886394[b]	.7819927[c]	.8895761[b]
	(.3793292)	(.3483344)	(.3338053)	(.3195122)
dnatcon[a]	.8606758[b]	.9159436[b]	.8594573[b]	.9154115[b]
	(.3206492)	(.3003448)	(.3206432)	(.299131)
dprojfin[a]	−.9738015[b]		1.048723[b]	
	(.2921523)		(.2702647)	
ncon	−.0092546[b]	−.0070053[b]	.0094014[b]	−.0070259[b]
	(.0029525)	(.0025353)	(.0029816)	(.0024907)
_cons	.1611176	−.7555456	.3181679	−.7537374
	(.9157232)	(.7805705)	(.8879077)	(.780066)

Note: Standard errors are shown in parentheses.
a. Denotes binary variables.
b. Coefficient significant at the 1 percent level.
c. Coefficient significant at the 5 percent level.

Table A3.2 *Marginal Effects of Independent Variables*

dreneg	M1 dF/dx	M2 dF/dx	M3 dF/dx	M4 dF/dx
gdp	.0000131	.0000579	8.50e–06	.0000576
	(.0000259)	(.0000268)	(.0000245)	(.0000263)
daward[a]	–.258637[b]	–.4237536[b]	–.2817683[b]	–.4236109[b]
	(.0783724)	(.0606156)	(.0686403)	(.0571005)
compet[a]	.1653906[b]			
	(.0546309)			
condur	–.0121341[b]	–.0147692[b]	–.0116443[b]	–.0147238[b]
	(.0018164)	(.0017818)	(.0016778)	(.0017243)
invest	.0003354[b]	.0002067[c]	.000342[c]	.0002067[c]
	(.0001033)	(.0000916)	(.0001024)	(.0000885)
dreg[a]	.162644[c]	.0872796	.1542887[c]	.0871531
	(.0629737)	(.0758451)	(.0618058)	(.0754238)
dgovguar[a]	.0679533	.0016584		
	(.0966497)	(.0748543)		
rbexist1[a]	–.5195089[b]	–.4915736[b]	–.5306469[b]	–.4915176[b]
	(.1315022)	(.1190138)	(.1297406)	(.1193189)
rbmin[a]	.3069235[b]	.3453243[b]	.3052453[b]	.3436941[b]
	(.0663767)	(.0621447)	(.06536)	(.0618188)
dtarreg2[a]	.1597149[c]	.2223604[b]	.1772397[c]	.2218473[b]
	(.0709781)	(.0608985)	(.0579388)	(.056287)
dnatcon[a]	.1999267[b]	.2350776[b]	.196488[b]	.2339195[b]
	(.0557199)	(.0553841)	(.0546241)	(.054885)
dprojfin[a]	–.3447597[b]		–.3703812[b]	
	(.1097618)		(.1016154)	
ncon	–.0028625[b]	–.0023737[b]	–.0028739[b]	–.0023739[b]
	(.0009078)	(.0008637)	(.0009048)	(.0008462)

Note: Standard errors are shown in parentheses.

a. Denotes binary variable, and *dF/dx* is for discrete change of dummy variable from 0 to 1, and it refers to the marginal probabilities of renegotiation induced by the respective variable.

b. Coefficient significant at the 1 percent level.

c. Coefficient significant at the 5 percent level.

Table A3.3 *The Impact of Corruption on Renegotiation Incidence*

Independent variables	Coefficients
gdp	0.0034[a]
	(2.52)
corrupt	0.55[a]
	(3.53)
rbexist1	−1.47[a]
	(−7.65)
rbmin	1.39[a]
	(8.95)
N	391

a. Significant variable at 5 percent level.

firms would prefer price-cap regulation, which is more risky but would allow these firms to get higher rents. Self-selection, however, may also lead one to think that riskier projects would be regulated by lower powered (cost plus) schemes. Finally, the type of financing that prevails cannot be considered as exogenous either, because private operators would be more willing to finance projects that appear as less risky or more profitable.

Second is an ex post moral hazard problem. Once the contract has been signed, the firm and the government would act strategically given the nature of this contract. Facing shorter contracts, firms might be induced to behave more efficiently to increase their chance to be awarded the contract again later on. Conversely, when protected by minimum income guarantee, they might make less effort. Price caps or private financing can also be expected to have incentive effects on the behavior of firms.

The problem to tackle is to disentangle these two dimensions to assess the real incentive effect of each specific aspect of the contract. That can be done through the use of a two-stage process aimed at controlling the self-selection effect of each of the variables suspected to be endogenous. To do this, one needs to find suitable instruments. Those instruments can be sectors, corruption, bureaucratic quality, rule of law, and existence of regulatory body, all of which are obviously exogenous in the sense that they are not determined by the risk of potential renegotiations. Nevertheless, finding instrumental variables that would not enter the equation to explain the probability of renegotiation appears very difficult, because virtually any contract characteristic and any aspect of the institutional and macroeconomic environment can be argued to have an impact on the probability of renegotiation. That exercise, accounting for the endogenous nature, is

undertaken in Guasch, Laffont, and Straub (2003) for operator-led renegotiations, and illustrates the robustness of most of the results.

Complete Estimates

Tables A3.4 through A3.15 present the complete econometric results of the four
estimated models, along with a correlation matrix of the main variables, plus
an additional estimation of the impact of the award process on renegotiation.

Table A3.4 Correlation Matrix of the Variables

(corr, dreneg, gdp, daward, multcrit, condur, invest, dreg, dgovguar, rbexist1, rbmin,
dtarreg2, dnatcon, dprojfin, ncon)
(observations = 372)

Variable	dreneg	gdp	daward	multcrit	condur	invest	dreg
dreneg	1.0000						
gdp	−0.0364	1.0000					
daward	−0.0543	0.4004	1.0000				
multcrit	0.0177	0.0403	0.4376	1.0000			
condur	−0.3943	−0.0184	−0.3647	−0.2728	1.0000		
invest	0.2297	0.1426	−0.0348	−0.0652	−0.1721	1.0000	
dreg	−0.1525	0.0571	0.1209	−0.0922	0.2218	0.0674	1.0000
dgovguar	0.1114	−0.1756	−0.6352	−0.1585	0.3952	0.0368	−0.1500
rbexist1	−0.3383	−0.2887	−0.4049	−0.1733	0.2081	0.0218	−0.1115
rbmin	0.3537	−0.3779	−0.1234	0.2102	0.1824	−0.0823	−0.1100
dtarreg2	−0.0171	0.3750	0.1822	0.1154	0.1207	0.0485	−0.0288
dnatcon	0.1498	0.0806	0.0448	−0.0786	0.1555	−0.0009	0.1215
dprojfin	−0.4399	0.0767	0.1816	0.1323	0.2243	−0.2246	0.4099
ncon	−0.2975	0.0925	0.0558	0.1677	−0.2711	0.0345	0.2027

	dgovguar	rbexist1	rbmin	dtarreg2	dnatcon	dprojfin	ncon
dgovguar	1.0000						
rbexist1	0.2165	1.0000					
rbmin	0.2221	−0.1662	1.0000				
dtarreg2	0.2042	−0.0522	−0.1594	1.0000			
dnatcon	−0.0886	−0.0610	0.1510	−0.0025	1.0000		
dprojfin	−0.2863	−0.1361	−0.1627	−0.0558	−0.0552	1.0000	
ncon	−0.1266	0.1555	−0.5773	0.1255	−0.2513	0.1929	1.0000

Note: This table presents the correlation matrix for the complete dataset of the variables
used here and indicates how different determinants of the incidence of renegotiation hang
together.

Table A3.5 *Estimates in M1*

(probit, dreneg, gdp, daward, multcrit, condur, invest, dreg, dgovguar, rbexist1, rbmin, dtarreg2, dnatcon, dprojfin, ncon)

Probit estimates	Number of observations = 372
	LR chi2(13) = 277.09
	Probability > chi2 = 0.0000
Log likelihood = –103.40189	Pseudo R2 = 0.5726

dreneg	Coefficient	Standard error	z	P > |z|	[95% Confidence interval]	
gdp	.0000423	.0000837	0.505	0.613	–.0001218	.0002063
daward	–.9830498	.3352856	–2.932	0.003	–1.640197	–.3259021
multcrit	.0252056	.3023747	0.083	0.934	–.567438	.6178492
condur	–.0392298	.0066922	–5.862	0.000	–.0523462	–.0261134
invest	.0010844	.000333	3.256	0.001	.0004317	.0017371
dreg	.6310063	.2836421	2.225	0.026	.075078	1.186935
dgovguar	.2220923	.3168987	0.701	0.483	–.3990177	.8432024
rbexist1	–1.423997	.3936929	–3.617	0.000	–2.195621	–.6523732
rbmin	1.316816	.3781053	3.483	0.000	.5757429	2.057889
dtarreg2	.6578784	.3793292	1.734	0.083	–.0855931	1.40135
dnatcon	.8606758	.3206492	2.684	0.007	.2322149	1.489137
dprojfin	–.9738015	.2921523	–3.333	0.001	–1.546409	–.4011935
ncon	–.0092546	.0029525	–3.135	0.002	–.0150414	–.0034679
_cons	.1611176	.9157232	0.176	0.860	–1.633667	1.955902

Table A3.6 *Marginal Effects: M1*

(*dprobit, dreneg, gdp, daward, multcrit, condur, invest, dreg, dgovguar, rbexist1, rbmin, dtarreg2, dnatcon, dprojfin, ncon*)

Probit estimates

Log likelihood = –103.40189

Number of observations = 372
LR chi2(13) = 277.09
Probability > chi2 = 0.0000
Pseudo R2 = 0.5726

dreneg	dF/dx	Standard error	z	P > |z|	x-bar	[95% Confidence interval]	
gdp	.0000131	.0000259	0.51	0.613	4,596.83	–.000038	.000064
daward[a]	–.258637	.0783724	–2.93	0.003	.306452	–.412244	–.10503
multcrit[a]	.0078451	.0946559	0.08	0.934	.150538	–.177677	.193367
condur	–.0121341	.0018164	–5.86	0.000	38.3301	–.015694	–.008574
invest	.0003354	.0001033	3.26	0.001	176.548	.000133	.000538
dreg[a]	.162644	.0629737	2.22	0.026	.846774	.039218	.28607
dgovguar[a]	.0679533	.0966497	0.70	0.483	.561828	–.121477	.257383
rbexist1[a]	–.5195089	.1315022	–3.62	0.000	.905914	–.777248	–.261769
rbmin[a]	.3069235	.0663767	3.48	0.000	.747312	.176828	.437019
dtarreg2[a]	.1597149	.0709781	1.73	0.083	.930108	.0206	.298829
dnatcon[a]	.1999267	.0557199	2.68	0.007	.88172	.090718	.309136
dprojfin[a]	–.3447597	.1097618	–3.33	0.001	.803763	–.559889	–.12963
ncon	–.0028625	.0009078	–3.13	0.002	43.2688	–.004642	–.001083

observed. *P* .3548387
predicted. *P* .237797 (at x-bar)

Note: z and P > \|z\| are tests of the underlying coefficient being 0.
a. *dF/dx* is for discrete change of the dummy variable from 0 to 1.

Table A3.7 *Estimates in M2: Dropping Project Finance*

(probit, dreneg, gdp, daward, multcrit, condur, invest, dreg, dgovguar, rbexist1, rbmin, dtarreg2, dnatcon, ncon)

Probit estimates   Number of observations = 422

LR chi2(12) = 281.49

Probability > chi2 = 0.0000

Log likelihood = −140.28005   Pseudo R2 = 0.5008

dreneg	Coefficient	Standard error	z	P > |z|	[95% Confidence interval]	
gdp	.0001708	.0000789	2.164	0.030	.0000161	.0003255
daward	−1.585373	.2688994	−5.896	0.000	−2.112406	−1.05834
multcrit	−.1149253	.2715943	−0.423	0.672	−.6472405	.4173898
condur	−.0435871	.0061395	−7.099	0.000	−.0556203	−.0315538
invest	.0006101	.0002696	2.263	0.024	.0000818	.0011385
dreg	.2711393	.2487905	1.090	0.276	−.2164811	.7587597
dgovguar	.0048946	.2209425	0.022	0.982	−.4281447	.437934
rbexist1	−1.322838	.3671021	−3.603	0.000	−2.042345	−.6033307
rbmin	1.3559	.3321795	4.082	0.000	.7048404	2.00696
dtarreg2	.886394	.3483344	2.545	0.011	.2036712	1.569117
dnatcon	.9159436	.3003448	3.050	0.002	.3272787	1.504609
ncon	−.0070053	.0025353	−2.763	0.006	−.0119745	−.0020362
_cons	−.7555456	.7805705	−0.968	0.333	−2.285436	.7743444

Table A3.8 *Marginal Effects: M2*

(*dprobit, dreneg, gdp, daward, multcrit, condur, invest, dreg, dgovguar, rbexist1, rbmin, dtarreg2, dnatcon, ncon*)

Probit estimates   Number of observations = 422
                                LR chi2(12) = 281.49
                                Probability > chi2 = 0.0000
Log likelihood = −140.28005   Pseudo R2 = 0.5008

dreneg	*dF/dx*	*Standard error*	*z*	*P > |z|*	*x–bar*	*[95% Confidence interval]*	
gdp	.0000579	.0000268	2.16	0.030	4,617.73	5.3e–06	.00011
daward[a]	−.4237536	.0606156	−5.90	0.000	.317536	−.542558	−.304949
multcrit[a]	−.0379794	.0874073	−0.42	0.672	.137441	−.209294	.133336
condur	−.0147692	.0017818	−7.10	0.000	36.5967	−.018262	−.011277
invest	.0002067	.0000916	2.26	0.024	186.732	.000027	.000386
dreg[a]	.0872796	.0758451	1.09	0.276	.798578	−.061374	.235933
dgovguar[a]	.0016584	.0748543	0.02	0.982	.528436	−.145053	.14837
rbexist1[a]	−.4915736	.1190138	−3.60	0.000	.917062	−.724836	−.258311
rbmin[a]	.3453243	.0621447	4.08	0.000	.767773	.223523	.467126
dtarreg2[a]	.2223604	.0608985	2.54	0.011	.938389	.103002	.341719
dnatcon[a]	.2350776	.0553841	3.05	0.002	.895735	.126527	.343628
ncon	−.0023737	.0008637	−2.76	0.006	43.3389	−.004067	−.000681

observed. *P* .3838863
predicted. *P* .2838467 (at x–bar)

Note: z and *P > |z|* are tests of the underlying coefficient being 0.
a. *dF/dx* is for discrete change of the dummy variable from 0 to 1.

Table A3.9 *Estimates in M3: Dropping Government Guarantee*

(*probit, dreneg, gdp, daward, multcrit, condur, invest, dreg, rbexist1, rbmin, dtarreg2, dnatcon, dprojfin, ncon*)

Probit estimates

Number of observations = 373
LR chi2(12) = 277.46
Probability > chi2 = 0.0000

Log likelihood = −103.6541   Pseudo R2 = 0.5724

dreneg	Coefficient	Standard error	z	P > |z|	[95% Confidence interval]	
gdp	.0000278	.0000803	0.346	0.729	0.000	.0001853
daward	−1.108564	.2853372	−3.885	0.000	−1.667815	−.5493138
multcrit	.0753693	.2929118	0.257	0.797	−.4987272	.6494659
condur	−.038092	.0064622	−5.895	0.000	−.0507577	−.0254263
invest	.0011189	.0003331	3.359	0.001	.0004661	.0017717
dreg	.6020085	.2788054	2.159	0.031	.05556	1.148457
rbexistl	−1.460583	.3921621	−3.724	0.000	−2.229207	−.6919594
rbmin	1.336007	.3793908	3.521	0.000	.5924149	2.079599
dtarreg2	.7819927	.3338053	2.343	0.019	.1277463	1.436239
dnatcon	.8594573	.3206432	2.680	0.007	.2310083	1.487906
dprojfin	−1.048723	.2702647	−3.880	0.000	−1.578433	−.5190142
dcon	−.0094014	.0029816	−3.153	0.002	−.0152452	−.0035576
_cons	.3181679	.8879077	0.358	0.720	−1.422099	2.058435

Table A3.10 *Marginal Effects: M3*

(*dprobit, dreneg, gdp, daward, multcrit, condur, invest, dreg, rbexist1, rbmin, dtarreg2, dnatcon, dprojfin, ncon*)

Probit estimates	Number of observations = 373
	LR chi2(12) = 277.46
	Probability > chi2 = 0.0000
Log likelihood = −103.6541	Pseudo R2 = 0.5724

dreneg	dF/dx	Standard error	z	P > |z|	x–bar	[95% Confidence interval]	
gdp	8.50e-06	.0000245	0.35	0.729	4,596.44	−.00004	.000057
daward[a]	−.2817683	.0686403	−3.89	0.000	.308311	−.416301	−.147236
multcrit[a]	−.2817683	.0928363	0.26	0.797	.150134	−.15848	.205432
condur	−.0116443	.0016778	−5.89	0.000	38.3614	−.014933	−.008356
invest	.000342	.0001024	3.36	0.001	176.389	.000141	.000543
dreg[a]	.1542887	.0618058	2.16	0.031	.847185	.033152	.275426
rbexist1[a]	−.5306469	.1297406	−3.72	0.000	.906166	−.784934	−.27636
rbmin[a]	.3052453	.0653600	3.52	0.000	.747989	.177142	.433348
dtarreg2[a]	.1772397	.0579388	2.34	0.019	.930295	.063682	.290798
dnatcon[a]	.196488	.0546241	2.68	0.007	.882038	.089427	.303549
dprojfin[a]	−.3703812	.1016154	−3.88	0.000	.80429	−.569544	−.171219
ncon	−.0028739	.0009048	−3.15	0.002	43.5255	−.004647	−.0011

observed. *P* .3538874
predicted. *P* .2327789 (at x-bar)

Note: z and *P* > |*z*| are tests of the underlying coefficient being 0.
a. *dF/dx* is for discrete change of the dummy variable from 0 to 1.

Table A3.11 Estimates in M4: Dropping Government Guarantee
and Project Finance

(*probit, dreneg, gdp, daward, multcrit, condur, invest, dreg, rbexist1, rbmin, dtarreg2, dnatcon, ncon*)

Probit estimates   Number of observations = 423

LR chi2(11) = 282.44

Probability > chi2 = 0.0000

Log likelihood = –140.28561   Pseudo R2 = 0.5017

dreneg	*Coefficient*	*Standard error*	*z*	*P > |z|*	*[95% Confidence interval]*	
gdp	.0001705	.0000777	2.194	0.028	.0000182	.0003229
daward	–1.588311	.2471818	–6.426	0.000	–2.072779	–1.103844
multcrit	–.1134499	.269005	–0.422	0.673	–.64069	.4137903
condur	–.0435773	.006021	–7.238	0.000	–.0553783	–.0317764
invest	.0006117	.0002612	2.342	0.019	.0000997	.0011237
dreg	.2716787	.2483975	1.094	0.274	–.2151714	.7585289
rbexist1	–1.322802	.3670613	–3.604	0.000	–2.042228	–.6033746
rbmin	1.355659	.3312332	4.093	0.000	.7064542	2.004864
dtarreg2	.8895761	.3195122	2.784	0.005	.2633437	1.515809
dnatcon	.9154115	.299131	3.060	0.002	.3291256	1.501697
ncon	–.0070259	.0024907	–2.821	0.005	–.0119076	–.0021442
_cons	–.7537374	.780066	–0.966	0.334	–2.282639	.7751638

Table A3.12 *Marginal Effects: M4*

(*dprobit, dreneg, gdp, daward, multcrit, condur, invest, dreg, rbexist1, rbmin, dtarreg2, dnatcon, ncon*)

Probit estimates

Number of observations = 423
LR chi2(11) = 282.44
Probability > chi2 = 0.0000
Log likelihood = –140.28561   Pseudo R2 = 0.5017

dreneg	dF/dx	Standard error	z	P > |z|	x–bar	[95% Confidence interval]	
gdp	.0000576	.0000263	2.19	0.028	4,617.35	6.0e-06	.000109
daward[a]	–.4236109	.0571005	–6.43	0.000	.319149	–.535526	–.311696
multcrit[a]	–.0373889	.0863514	–0.42	0.673	.137116	–.206634	.131857
condur	–.0147238	.0017243	–7.24	0.000	36.6284	–.018103	–.011344
invest	.0002067	.0000885	2.34	0.019	186.567	.000033	.00038
dreg[a]	.0871531	.0754238	1.09	0.274	.799054	–.060675	.234981
rbexist1[a]	–.4915176	.1193189	–3.60	0.000	.917258	–.725378	–.257657
rbmin[a]	.3436941	.0618188	4.09	0.000	.768322	.222531	.464857
dtarreg2[a]	.2218473	.056287	2.78	0.005	.938534	.111527	.332168
dnatcon[a]	.2339195	.054885	3.06	0.002	.895981	.126347	.341492
ncon	–.0023739	.0008462	–2.82	0.005	43.565	–.004032	–.000715

observed. *P* .3829787
predicted. *P* .2821616 (at x-bar)

Note: z and P > \|z\| are tests of the underlying coefficient being 0.
a. *dF/dx* is for discrete change of the dummy variable from 0 to 1.

Table A3.13 *Estimates in the Award Process*

(*dprobit, dreneg, gdp, dcp_bid, daward, multcrit, condur, drbauto, texp*)

Probit estimates

Number of observations = 610
LR chi2 (7) = 637.43
Probability > chi2 = 0.0000

Log likelihood = –221.45967   Pseudo R2 = 0.4534

dreneg	Coefficient	Standard error	z	P > |z|	[95% Confidence interval]	
gdp	.00033[a]	.0000555	5.949	0.000	0.0002212	.0004387
dcp_bid	.567126[a]	.2082842	2.723	0.006	.1588966	.9753555
daward	–.9775542[a]	.1679535	–5.820	0.000	–1.306737	–.6483714
multcrit	–.3759041[b]	.208067	–1.807	0.071	–.783708	.0318998
condur	–.0156244[c]	.0062874	–2.485	0.013	–.0279474	–.0033014
drbauto	–1.860391[a]	.2399469	–7.753	0.000	–2.330678	–1.390104
texp	–.1460424[a]	.0239522	–6.097	0.000	–.1929877	–.099097
_cons	–.1802966	.2849076	–0.633	0.527	–.7387052	.3781119

a. Significant at the 1 percent level.
b. Significant at the 10 percent level.
c. Significant at the 5 percent level.

Table A3.14 *Marginal Effects: Award Process*

(*dprobit, dreneg, gdp, dcp_bid, daward, multcrit, condur, drbauto, texp*)

Probit estimates   Number of observations = 610

LR chi2 (7) = 637.43

Probability > chi2 = 0.0000

Log likelihood = –221.45967   Pseudo R2 = 0.4534

dreneg	dF/dx	Standard error	z	P > |z|	x–bar	[95% Confidence interval]	
gdp	.0001052	.0000187	5.95	0.000	4,311.37	.000069	.000142
dcp_bid[a]	.1653906	.0546309	2.72	0.006	.704918	.058316	.272465
daward[a]	–.2591174	.0426194	–5.82	0.000	.268852	–.34265	–.175585
multcrit[a]	–.1074875	.0521677	–1.81	0.071	.114754	–.209734	–.005241
condur	–.0049839	.0018175	–2.49	0.013	35.5357	–.008546	–.001422
drbauto[a]	–.4551609	.0494435	–7.75	0.000	.337705	–.552068	–.358253
texp	–.046585	.0081091	–6.10	0.000	5.62459	–.062479	–.030691

observed. *P* .3803279

predicted. *P* .2517963 (at x-bar)

Note: z and P > |z| are tests of the underlying coefficient being 0.

a. *dF/dx* is for discrete change of the dummy variable from 0 to 1.

Table A3.15 *Correlation Matrix*

(*corr, dreneg, gdp, dcp_bid, daward, multcrit, condur, drbauto, texp*)
(observations = 610)

	dreneg	gdp	dcp_bid	daward	multcrit	condur	drbauto
dreneg	1.0000						
gdp	0.1157	1.0000					
dcp_bid	0.3292	0.3062	1.0000				
daward	−0.1247	0.3539	0.3842	1.0000			
multcrit	−0.0278	0.0506	0.2329	0.3849	1.0000		
condur	−0.3778	−0.0570	−0.5997	−0.2572	−0.2087	1.0000	
drbauto	−0.4809	0.3028	−0.2752	−0.0655	−0.2353	0.5207	1.0000
texp	−0.3934	−0.0576	−0.1224	0.0264	0.0982	0.0707	0.1617

References

The word "processed" denotes informally produced works that my not be readily available through libraries.

Aghion, Phillip, Mathias Dewatripont, and P. Rey. 1994. "Renegotiation Design with Unverifiable Information." *Econometrica* 62(2): 257–82.

Alexander, A., C. Mayer, and M. Weeds. 1996. "Regulatory Structure and Risk and Infrastructure Firms: An International Comparison." Policy Research Working Paper no. 1698. World Bank, Washington, D.C.

Alexander, I., A. Estache, and A. Oliveri. 2001. "A Few Things Transport Regulators Should Know about Risk and the Cost of Capital." *Utilities Policy* 9: 12–25.

Anderlini, L., L. Felli, and A. Postlewaite. 2000. "Courts of Law, Unforeseen Contingencies and Incomplete Contracts." Northwestern University, Evanston, Ill., Processed.

Artana, D., F. Navajas, and J. Urbizondo. 1998. "Regulation and Contractual Adaptation in Public Utilities: The Case of Argentina." Technical Report. Inter-American Development Bank, Washington, D.C.

Aubert, C., and J. J. Laffont. 2002. "Political Renegotiation of Regulatory Contracts." Institute d'Economie Industrielle of Toulouse, Toulouse, France. Processed.

Bajari, P., and S. Tadelli. 2000. "Incentives versus Transaction Costs: A Theory of Procurement Contracts." Processed.

Banerjee, Abhijit, and Ester Duflo. 2002. "Reputation Effects and the Limits of Contracting: A Study of the Indian Software Industry." *Quarterly Journal of Economics* 54: 82–103.

Barja, Gover, David McKenzie, and Miguel Urquiola. 2002. "Capitalization and Privatization in Bolivia. Cornell University, Ithaca, N.Y. Processed.

Battigalli, Pierpaolo, and Giovani Maggi. 2000. "Imperfect Contracting." Princeton University, Princeton, N.J. Processed.

Beato, Paulina, and J. J. Laffont. 2002. "Competition in Public Utilities in Developing Countries." Report no. IFM-127 Inter-American Development Bank, Washington, D.C.

Benitez, D., O. Chisari, and A. Estache. 2003. "Can the Gains from Argentina's Utilities Reform Offset Credit Shocks?" in C. Ugaz and C. Waddams Price, eds., *Utility Privatization and Regulation: A Fair Deal for Consumers?* Northampton, Mass.: Edward Elgar.

Benitez, D., A. Estache, M. Kennet, and C. Ruzzier. 2002. "The Potential Role of Economic Cost Models in the Regulation of Telecommunications in Developing Countries." *Information Economics and Policy* 14(1): 21–38.

Birdsall, Nancy, and John Nellis. 2002. "Winners and Losers: Assessing the Distributional Impact of Privatization." Working Paper no. 6. Center for Global Developments, Washington D.C.

Bitran, E., A. Estache, J. L. Guasch, and P. Serra. 1999. "Privatizing and Regulating Chile's Utilities, 1974–2000: Successes, Failures, and Outstanding Challenges." In G. Perry and D. Leipiziger, eds., *Chile: Recent Policy Lessons and Emerging Challenges.* World Bank Institute Development Studies. Washington, D.C.: World Bank.

Bondt, P. 2001. *A Theory of Contractual Incompleteness Based on Judicial Agency.* Evanston, Ill.: Northwestern University.

Bowersox, Donald M., and David J. Closs. 1996. *Logistical Management: The Integrated Supply Chain Process.* New York: McGraw-Hill.

Brook, Penelope J., and Timothy C. Irwin. 2003. *Infrastructure for Poor People: Public Policy for Private Provision.* Washington, D.C.: World Bank.

Calderon, Cesar, and Luis Serven. 2003. "The Growth Cost of Latin America's Infrastructure Gap." In William Easterly and Luis Serven, eds., *Adjustment Undermined? Infrastructure, Public Deficits and Growth in Latin America, 1980–2000.* Princeton, N.J.: Princeton University Press.

Calderon, Cesar, William Easterly, and Luis Serven. 2003a. "Infrastructure Compression and Public Sector Solvency in Latin America." In William Easterly and Luis Serven, eds., *Adjustment Undermined? Infrastructure, Public Deficits and Growth in Latin America, 1980–2000.* Princeton, N.J.: Princeton University Press.

———. 2003b. "Latin America's Infrastructure in the Era of Macroeconomics Crisis?" In William Easterly and Luis Serven, eds., *Adjustment Undermined? Infrastructure, Public Deficits and Growth in Latin America, 1980–2000.* Princeton, N.J.: Princeton University Press.

Campos, J., A. Estache, and L. Trujillo. 2003. "Processes and Accounting Matter for Regulators: Learning from Argentina's Railways Privatization." *Journal of Network Industries* 4(1): 3–27.

Canning, D. 1998. "A Database of World Infrastructure Stocks, 1950–95." Policy Research Working Paper no. 1929. World Bank, Washington, D.C.

Carey A., M. Cave, R. Duncan, G. Houston, and K. Langford. 1994. "Accounting for Regulation in UK Utilities." Center for the Study of Regulated Industries, Institute of Chartered Accountants in England and Wales, London.

Chisari, O., A. Estache, and C. Romero. 1999. "Winners and Losers from the Privatization and Regulation of Utilities: Lessons from a General Equilibrium Model of Argentina." *World Bank Economic Review* 13(2): 357–78.

Chung, Tai-Yeong. 1992. "On the Social Optimality of Liquidated Damage Clauses: An Economic Analysis." *Journal of Law, Economics, and Organizations* 8: 280–305.

———. 1995. "On Strategic Commitment: Contracting Versus Investment." *Papers and Proceedings of the American Economic Association* 85: 437–41.

Coelli, T., A. Estache, S. Perelman, and L. Trujillo. 2003. *A Primer on Efficiency Measurement for Utilities and Transport Regulators.* World Bank Institute Development Studies. Washington, D.C.: World Bank.

Dewatripont, Mathias. 1988. "Commitment through Renegotiation-Proof Contracts with Third Parties." *Review of Economic Studies* 55: 377–90.

Dornberger, Simon, Shirley Meadowcroft, and David Thompson. 1986. "Competitive Tendering and Efficiency: The Case of Refuse Collection." *Fiscal Studies* 7: 69–87.

Engel, Eduardo, R. Fischer, and Alexander Galetovic. 1996. "Licitación de Carreteras en Chile." *Estudios Públicos* 61: 5–37. Available on: http://www.cepchile.cl/cep/docs/61engel.pdf.

———. 1997a. "¿Cómo licitar una concesión vial urbana?" *Estudios Públicos* 67: 177–214. Available on: http://www.cepchile.cl/cep/docs/67engel.pdf.

———. 1997b. "Infrastructure Financing and Government Guarantees." In T. Irwin, M. Klein, G. Perry, and M. Thobani, eds., *Dealing with Public Risk in Private Infrastructure.* Washington, D.C.: World Bank.

———. 1998. "Least Present Value of Revenue Auctions and Highway Franchising." Working Paper no. 6889. National Bureau of Economic Research, Washington, D.C.

———. 2000. "Franchising of Infrastructure Concessions in Chile: A Policy Report." Discussion Paper. Universidad de Chile, Santiago, Chile.

———. 2001. "Least-Present-Value Revenue Auction and Highway Franchising." *Journal of Political Economy* 109(5): 993–1020.

———. 2003. "Highway Franchising in Latin America: Is This the Right Model?" Yale University, Economics Department, New Haven, Conn. Processed.

Ennis, Huberto, and Santiago Pinto. 2002. "Privatization and Income Distribution in Argentina." West Virginia University, Morgantown, W. Va. Processed.

Estache, A. 2003a. "Argentina Privatization: A Cure or a Disease?" in C. von Hirschhausen, ed., *Proceedings of a Workshop on Applied Infrastructure Research.* Berlin: Berlin University of Technology, School of Management and Technology.

———. 2003b."On Latin America's Infrastructure Privatization and Its Distributional Effects." Paper presented at the conference on the Distributional Consequences of Privatization, February 24–25, Center for Global Development, London.

Estache, Antonio, and G. de Rus, eds. 2000. *Privatization and Regulation of Transport Infrastructure: Guidelines for Policymakers and Regulators.* Studies in Development Series. Washington, D.C.: World Bank Institute.

Estache, Antonio, and Lucia Quesada. 2001. "Concession Contracts Renegotiation: The Efficiency and Equity Dilemma." Policy Research Working Paper no. 2705. World Bank, Washington, D.C.

Estache, Antonio, Vivien Foster, and Quentin Woodon. 2002. *Accounting for Poverty in Infrastructure Reform-Learning from the Latin America's Experience.* Studies in Development Series. Washington, D.C.: World Bank Institute.

Estache, A., A. Gomez-Lobo, and D. Leipziger. 2001. "Utilities Privatization and the Poor: Lessons and Evidence from Latin America." *World Development* 29(7): 1179–98.

Estache, A., M. Gonzalez, and L. Trujillo. 2002a. "Efficiency Gains from Port Reform and the Potential for Yardstick Competition: Lessons from Mexico." *World Development* 30(4): 545–60.

———. 2002b. "What Does Privatization Do for Efficiency? Evidence from Argentina's and Brazil's Railways." *World Development* 30(11): 1885–97.

Estache, Antonio, J. Luis Guasch, and Lourdes Trujillo. 2003. "Price Caps, Efficiency Payoffs and Infrastructure Renegotiation in Latin America." In *The UK Model of Regulation: A Retrospective of the 20 Years since the Littlechild Report.* London: London Business School Press.

Estache, A., M. Rodríguez-Pardina, J. M. Rodríguez, and G. Sember. 2002. "An Introduction to Financial and Economic Modeling for Utility Regulators." Policy Research Working Paper no 3001. World Bank, Washington, D.C.

Foster, Vivien, J. Luis Guasch, Maria Elena Pinglo, and Sophie Sirtaine. 2003. "Has Private Investment in Infrastructure in Latin America Been Profitable? An Empirical Analysis 1990—2000." World Bank, Washington, D.C. Processed.

Freije, Samuel, and Luis Rivas. 2003. "Privatization, Inequality, and Welfare: Evidence from Nicaragua." Center for Global Development, Washington, D.C. Processed.

Fundación de Investigaciones Económicas Latinoamericanas. 1999. *La Regulación de la Competencia y de los Servicios Públicos: Teoría y Experiencia Argentina Reciente.* Buenos Aires.

Gomez-Ibanez, J. A. 2003. *Regulation of Private Infrastructure: Monopoly, Contracts, and Discretion.* Cambridge, Mass.: Harvard University Press.

Gordon, M. J., and E. Shapiro. 1956. "Capital Equipment Analysis: The Required Rate of Profit." *Management Science* 3(October): 102–10.

Green, J., and Jean-Jacques Laffont. 1992. "Renegotiation and the Form of Efficient Contracts." *Annales d'Economie et de Statistique* 25/26: 123–50.

Green, R., and M. Rodriguez-Pardina. 1999. *Resetting Price Controls for Privatized Utilities: A Manual for Regulators.* World Bank Institute Studies in Development. Washington, D.C.: World Bank.

Guasch, J. Luis. 2002. *Logistic Costs and Their Impact and Determinants in Latin America and the Caribbean.* Washington, D.C.: World Bank.

———. 2003. "Infrastructure Concessions in Latin America and the Caribbean: The Renegotiation Issue and Its Determinants." *Infrastructure and Financial Markets Review* 9(2): 1–6.

Guasch, J. Luis, and Robert Hahn. 1999. "The Costs and Benefits of Regulation: Implications for Developing Countries." *World Bank Research Observer* 14(1): 137–58.

Guasch, J. Luis, and Joseph Kogan. 2001. "Inventories in Developing Countries: Levels and Determinants—A Red Flag for Competitiveness and Growth." Working Paper no. 2552. World Bank, Washington, D.C.

———. 2003. "Just-in-Case Inventories." Working Paper no. 3012. World Bank, Washington, D.C.

Guasch, J. Luis, and Pablo Spiller. 1999. *Managing the Regulatory Process: Design, Concepts, Issues and the Latin America and Caribbean Story.* Washington, D.C.: World Bank.

———. 2001. *The Challenge of Designing and Implementing Effective Regulation: A Normative Approach and an Empirical Evaluation.* Washington, D.C.: World Bank.

Guasch, J. Luis, Luis Andres, and Vivien Foster. Forthcoming. "Performance of Latin America and Caribbean Infrastructure Reform Programs: Determinants of Success and Failure." World Bank, Washington, D.C. Processed.

Guasch, J. Luis, A. Kartacheva, and Lucia Quesada. 2000. *Contract Renegotiations and Concessions in the Latin America and Caribbean Region: An Economic Analysis and Empirical Implications.* Washington, D.C.: World Bank.

Guasch, J. Luis, Jean-Jacques Laffont, and Stephane Straub. 2003. "Renegotiation of Concession Contracts in Latin America." Policy Research Working Paper no. 3011. World Bank, Washington, D.C.

Harris, Clive. 2002. *The Beginning of the End or the End of the Beginning? A Review of Private Participation in Infrastructure in Developing Countries.* Washington, D.C.: World Bank.

Hart, Oliver, and J. Moore. 1988. "Incomplete Contracts and Renegotiation." *Econometrica* 56: 755–85.

Hughes, Gordon. 1999. *Lessons from Private Sector Concessions.* Washington, D.C.: World Bank.

Jeon, D. S., and Jean-Jacques Laffont. 1999 "Renegotiation of Concession Contracts: A Theoretical Framework." World Bank, Washington, D.C. Processed.

Kaufmann, Daniel, Aart Kraay, and Pablo Zoido-Lobaton. 1999a. "Aggregating Governance Indicators." Policy Research Working Paper no. 2195. World Bank, Washington, D.C.

———. 1999b. "Governance Matters." Policy Research Working Paper no. 2196. Washington, D.C.: World Bank.

Kerf, Michel, R. David Gray, Timothy Irwin, Celine Levesque, and Robert Taylor. 1998. "Concessions for Infrastructure: A Guide to Their Design and Award." Technical Paper no. 389. Washington, D.C.: World Bank.

Kikeri, Sunita, and John Nellis. 2002. "Privatization in Competitive Sectors: The Record to Date." Policy Research Working Paper no. 2860. World Bank, Washington, D.C.

Klein, Michael. 1998a. "Bidding for Concessions: How Contract Design Affects Competition and Contract Sustainability." In *Public Policy for the Private Sector.* View Point no. 158. Washington, D.C.: World Bank, Finance, Private Sector, and Infrastructure Network.

———. 1998b. "The Case for Periodic Rebidding of Concessions." In *Public Policy for the Private Sector.* View Point no. 159. Washington, D.C.: World Bank, Finance, Private Sector, and Infrastructure Network.

———. 1998c. "Designing Auctions for Concessions: Guessing the Right Value to Bid and the Winner's Curse." In *Public Policy for the Private Sector.* View Point no. 160. Washington, D.C.: World Bank, Finance, Private Sector, and Infrastructure Network.

———. 1998d. "Infrastructure Concessions: To Auction or Negotiate?" In *Public Policy for the Private Sector.* View Point no. 161. Washington, D.C.: World Bank, Finance, Private Sector, and Infrastructure Network.

Knack, Stephen, and Philip Keefer. 1995. "Institutions and Economic Performance: Cross Country Tests Using Alternative Institutional Measures." *Economics and Politics* 7(3): 207–27.

Laffont, Jean-Jacques. 2000. *Incentives and Political Economy.* Oxford, U.K.: Oxford University Press.

———. 2001. "Enforcement, Regulation and Development." Paper presented at the conference of the African Economic Research Council, May 20–22, Nairobi.

———. 2002. *Regulation and Development.* Caffe Lecture. Rome: University of La Sapienza.

Laffont, J. J., and D. Martimort. 2002. *The Theory of Incentives.* Princeton, N.J.: Princeton University Press.

Laffont, Jean-Jacques, and M. Meleu. 2001. "Enforcement of Contracts with Adverse Selection in LDCs." Institut d'Economie Industrielle, Toulouse, France. Processed.

Laffont, Jean-Jacques, and Jean Tirole. 1993. *A Theory of Incentives in Procurement and Regulation.* Cambridge, Mass.: Massachusetts Institute of Technology Press.

La Porta, Rafael, and Florencio Lopez-de-Silanes. 1999. "The Benefits of Privatization: Evidence from Mexico." *Quarterly Journal of Economics* 114(4): 1193–1242.

Lopez-Calva, Luis Felipe, and Juan Rosellon. 2002. "The Benefits of Privatization: Evidence from México." Universidad de las Americas, Puebla, Mexico. Processed.

Macedo, Roberto. 2000. "Privatization and the Distribution of Assets and Income in Brazil." Working Paper no 14. Carnegie Endowment for International Peace, Washington, D.C.

Manelli, Alejandro M., and Daniel R. Vincent. 1995. "Optional Procurement Mechanisms." *Econometrica* 63(3): 591–620.

Manzetti, L., ed. 2000. *Regulatory Policy in Latin America: Post-Privatization Realities.* Miami, Fla.: University of Miami, North-South Press Center.

McAfee, R. Preston, and John McMillan. 1986. "Bidding for Contracts: A Principal Agent Analysis." *Rand Journal of Economics* 17(3):326–38.

McKenzie, David, and Dilip Mookherjee. 2003. "Distributive Impact of Privatization in Latin America: An Overview of Evidence from Four Countries." *Economia* 3(2): 161–233.

Megginson, W. L., and J. Netter. 2001. "From State to Market: A Survey of Empirical Studies on Privatization." *Journal of Economic Literature* 39(2, June): 321–89.

Mueller, B. 2001. "Institutions for Commitment in the Brazilian Regulatory System." *Quarterly Review of Economics and Finance* 41(5): 621–43.

Navajas, F. 2000. "El impacto distributivo de los cambios en los precios relativos en la Argentina entre 1988–1998 y los efectos de las privatizaciones y la desregulación económica." In *La Distribucion del Ingreso en la Argentina.* Buenos Aires: Fundación de Investigaciones Económicas Latinoamericanas.

Nellis, John. 2003. "Privatization in Africa: What Has Happened? What Is to be Done?" Working Paper no. 25. Center for Global Development, Washington, D.C.

Newbery, David M. 2000. *Privatization, Restructuring and Regulation of Network Utilities.* Cambridge, Mass.: Massachusetts Institute of Technology Press.

Pritchett, Lant H. 2000. "The Tyranny of Concepts: CUDIE (Cumulated, Depreciated, Investment Effort) Is Not Capital." Policy Research Working Paper no. 2341. World Bank, Washington, D.C.

Reinikka, Ritva, and Jakob Svensson. 1999. "How Inadequate Provision of Public Infrastructure and Services Affect Private Investment." Policy Research Working Paper no. 2262. World Bank, Washington, D.C.

Ross, S., R. Westerfield, and J. Jaffe. 1999. *Corporate Finance*, 5th ed. New York: Irwin McGraw-Hill.

Segal, I., and M. Whinston. 2002. "The Mirrlees Approach to Mechanism Design with Renegotiation (with applications to Hold-Up and Risk Sharing)." *Econometrica* 70(1): 1–46.

Smith, Warrick. 1997a. "Utility Regulators—Decisionmaking Structures, Resources and Start-up Strategy." *Viewpoint* 129. World Bank, Washington, D.C.

————. 1997b. "Utility Regulators—The Independence Debate." *Viewpoint* 127. World Bank, Washington, D.C.

————. 1997c. "Utility Regulators—Roles and Responsibilities." *Viewpoint* 128. World Bank, Washington, D.C.

Spiller, P. T. 1993. "Institutions and Regulatory Commitment in Utilities' Privatization." *Industrial and Corporate Change* 2(3): 387–450.

Tirole, Jean. 1986. "Procurement and Renegotiation." *Journal of Political Economy* 94(2): 235–59.

————. 1999. "Incomplete Contracts: Where Do We Stand?" *Econometrica* 67: 741–81.

Torero, Maximo, and Alberto Pasco-Font. 2001. "The Social Impact of Privatization and Regulation of Utilities in Peru."Discussion Paper no. 2001/17. Stockholm: World Institute for Development Economics Research.

Ugaz, C., and C. Waddams-Price, eds. 2003. *Utility Privatization and Regulation and Regulation: A Fair Deal for Consumers?* Northampton, Mass.: Edward Elgar Press.

World Bank. 1994. *Infrastructure for Development: World Development Report 1994.* Oxford University Press: New York.

Index

Accounting, regulatory, 129–134
Arbitration rules, 135
Argentina
    devaluation in, 65
    re-bid in power sector in, 28
    water and sanitation services in, 45,
        53–54, 62–63
Asset valuation
    concession termination and, 126–127
    elements of, 121, 125–126
Awards process. *See* Concession awards

Bids
    problems due to aggressive, 44–48
    renegotiation and, 34–35, 37–39, 41,
        107
    strategic under-, 36–37, 39
Bolivia, 60
BOT projects
    in Colombia, 55
    financing, 30–31
    in Mexico, 62
Brazil, 60–61
Buenos Aires, Argentina, 45, 53–54

Caribbean
    concessions in, 80
    economic reforms in, 23
    level and quality of infrastructure in,
        2–3
    renegotiated concessions in, 82, 86
    renegotiation issues in, 77–78

Cellular phone contracts, 64
Cochabamba, Bolivia, 60
Colombia
    airport concession in, 54–55
    telecommunications concession in, 44
Concession awards
    municipal, 66–68
    optimal criteria for, 101–105
    optimal transfer fee and, 101, 104, 105
    process and criteria for, 97–102
    renegotiation and noncompetitive,
        13–15
Concession contracts
    arbitration rules in, 135
    conclusions regarding, 141–147
    duration of, 28
    elements of, 19–21, 27–30, 141
    financial equilibrium clauses in, 36,
        105–106
    incomplete, 71–77
    informational requirements in,
        127–128
    investment commitments and,
        108–109
    investor and user protections in, viii
    length and financing of, 107–108
    methods of awarding, 13–14
    rate of return vs. price cap regulation
        and, 111, 113–115
    regulatory oversight and, 27
    renegotiation and features of, 16–17
    renegotiation clauses in, 107

Concession design
  airport concession in Colombia, 54–55
  allocation of risk and, 121–125,
    143–144
  elements of faulty, 48–52, 144
  guidelines for optimal, 96–97
  Mexico's highway program, 52
  regulation and, 64–65, 144–145
  renegotiation and, 91–93, 95–96
  road concessions in Dominican
    Republic, 55–56
  telecommunications provider selection
    in Guatemala, 56–60
  water and sanitation concession in
    Buenos Aires, 53–54
  water and sanitation concession
    termination in Bolivia, 60
Concession fees, 100–101
Concession risk, 6–9, 121–125, 143–144
Concession termination
  in Bolivia, 60
  determining compensation for,
    126–127
  dispute resolution and, 134
Concessions
  abandoned, 45–46
  aggressive bidding and, 44
  asset valuation of, 121, 125–126
  background of, viii–ix
  benefits of, 31
  common mistakes in, 49–51
  contract features and incidence of, 16,
    85–86
  cost of capital and, 115–121
  data descriptions on, 149–156
  design of, 91–93
  directly adjudicated, 39–40
  drawbacks of, 31–33
  government responsibilities for, 29,
    40
  investment obligations of, 16, 92,
    108–109
  overview of, 9–13
  political and institutional issues and,
    44
  privatizations vs., 30–31
  problems with, 43–44
  regulation of, 15
  regulatory accounting norms for,
    129–134
  regulatory agencies and, 134–139
  regulatory design and, 32
  renegotiated, 46–48

Contingency clauses, 73
Contract renegotiation
  bidding and, 34–35, 37–39, 41
  concession design and, 40–41
  cost issues and, 41
  directly adjudicated concessions and,
    39–40
  examples of, 46–48
  financial equilibrium in regulated
    markets and, 35–37
  government-led, 40
  incentives for, 8
  incidence of, 12–13, 16–17, 33–35, 78,
    85–86
  incomplete contracts and, 71–77
  independent variables and, 157–166
  investment obligations and, 16, 92,
    108–109
  justified renegotiation for, 19–21
  macroeconomic shocks and, 41–42,
    88
  marginal effects on probability of, 90
  noncompetitive contract awards and,
    13–15
  outcomes of, 17–18
  proper use of, 19–20
  regulation and, 89, 91, 143
  theory of, 72–77
Contract renegotiation study
  basic findings of, 80–87
  empirical analysis of renegotiation
    determinants in, 87–88
  empirical results interpretation in,
    90–94
  overview of, 79
  variables influencing renegotiation
    incidence in, 88–90
Convertibility Law (Argentina), 65
Corruption, political, 93
Cost of capital
  method to determine, 115–119
  tariff and revenue implications of,
    120–121
Cost of equity
  explanation of, 118–119
  in Latin America, 120

Data descriptions, 149–156
Dispute resolution, 134
Dominican Republic
  power producers in, 48
  renegotiation in, 69
  road concessions in, 55–56

East Asia
  economic growth in, 2–3
  level and quality of infrastructure in, 2
Econometric analysis
  complete econometric results and,
    171–182
  summary results, 167–171
Economic growth, 2–6
El Dorado International Airport, 54
Elections, 93
Electricity generation, 23
Ex post penalties, 74

Financial advisors, 97
Financial equilibrium, 35–37
Financial equilibrium clauses, 36, 105–106
Financing, 89–90

Governments
  infrastructure service provision and,
    vii–viii, 1, 2
  objectives and commitment of, 72
  political constraints faced by, 77
  responsibilities for concessions, 29, 40
Guatemala, 56–60

Incomplete contracts. *See also* Concession
  contracts
  concession successes or failures and,
    72–77
  reasons for, 71–72
Independent variables, 157–166
India, 69
Indonesia, 68
Infrastructure firm betas, 111–113
Infrastructure reform programs
  performance delivery and, 9–13
  requirements for, 146–147
Infrastructure services
  government enterprises providing,
    vii–viii, 1, 2
  private participation of, 23, 24
  private sector transfer of, 26–27
Institutional issues, 44
Institutions theory, 76–77
Inventories, 3–6
Investment bankers, 97
Investment obligations, 16, 92, 108–109

Jamaica, 48

Latin America
  cost of equity in, 120
  economic reforms in, 23

level and quality of infrastructure in,
    2–3
  number of concessions in, 80
  number of renegotiated concessions in,
    82, 86
  price-cap regulation in, 113
  renegotiation issues in, 77–78
Lease payments, 100
Least present value of revenues (LPVR),
  104–105
Lima, Peru, 45, 47
Limeira, Brazil, 60–61
Logistics costs, 6, 7

Macroeconomic shocks
  impact of, 8–9, 65, 68–69
  renegotiation and, 41–42, 88
Mastec, 59–60
Matarani, Peru, 64
Mexico
  highway program in, 52
  railroad privatization in, 47–48
  water and sanitation concessions in,
    62
Minas Gerais, Brazil, 96
Municipal concessions, 66–68

Natural gas, 23

Optimal transfer fee, 101, 104
Outright privatization, 23, 24

Pakistan, 69
Performance delivery
  infrastructure reform programs and,
    9–13
  by private enterprises, 1–2
Peru
  concessions problems in, 44, 45–47
  port concession in, 64
Political influences
  concession problems due to, 44
  renegotiation probabilities and, 89,
    93–94
  types of, 77, 93–94
Prequalification, 26, 101–103
Price-cap regime, 15
Price-cap regulation, 111, 114–115
Private enterprises
  background of participation by, 23–25
  performance delivery by, 1–2
  profitability of, 11–12
  regulations and risks for, 6–9

Private infrastructure projects, 38
Private participation
    background of, 23–25
    concessions vs., 30–31
    types of, 23, 25

Rate-of-return regulation, 15, 111, 114–115
Regulation
    concession design and, 64–65, 96–97,
        144–145
    price-cap, 111, 114–115
    rate-of-return, 15, 111, 114–115
    renegotiation incidence and, 89, 91,
        143
    risk for private enterprises and,
        6–9
    role of, 15, 26, 32, 91
Regulatory accounting, 129–134
Regulatory agencies
    features of, 136–137
    function of, 135
    objectives of, 138–139
    user complaint procedures of, 138
Renegotiation. *See* Contract renegotiation
Risk. *See* Concession risk

Samana highway (Dominican Republic),
    55–56

Sanitation sector, 24, 34
Sector restructuring, 26, 97

Tariffs
    adjustment of, 60–61
    award criteria and, 98–99
    cost of capital implications and,
        120–121
    determining future, 109–111
    regulation constraints and, 35
    revision of, 110–111
Telecommunications sector, 23, 34
Termination. *See* Concession termination
Transaction costs, 73
Transfer fees, 101, 104, 105
Transportation sector
    concessions for, 24
    renegotiation in, 34, 114
Tucuman, Argentina, 62–63

Ukraine, 64
Unbundling, 26
Unit costs, 3
Uruguay, 44

Water and sanitation sector
    concessions for, 24
    renegotiation in, 34, 114